My *Victoria* CAST IRON TORTILLA PRESS *Cookbook*

101 SURPRISINGLY DELICIOUS HOMEMADE TORTILLA RECIPES WITH INSTRUCTIONS

BY

JULIE KNIGHT-WATERS

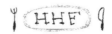

HHF PRESS

SAN FRANCISCO

Legal Notice

The information contained in this book is for entertainment purposes only. The content represents the opinion of the author and is based on the author's personal experience and observations. The author does not assume any liability whatsoever for the use of or inability to use any or all information contained in this book, and accepts no responsibility for any loss or damages of any kind that may be incurred by the reader as a result of actions arising from the use of information in this book. Use this information at your own risk.

The author reserves the right to make any changes he or she deems necessary to future versions of the publication to ensure its accuracy.

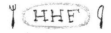

DO YOU LIKE FREE BOOKS?

Every month we release a new book, and we offer it to our current readers first...absolutely free! This helps us get early feedback before launching a book, and lets you stock your shelf full of interesting and valuable books for free!

Some recent titles include:

- The Complete Vegetable Spiralizer Cookbook
- My Lodge Cast Iron Skillet Cookbook
- 101 The New Crepes Cookbook

To receive this month's free book, just go to

http://www.healthyhappyfoodie.org/aa1-freebooks

Table Of Contents

1

Why You Need This Book!

The Most All-Inclusive Book on the Victoria Cast Iron Tortilla Press

Welcome to the wild, wonderful, and totally scrumptious world of super healthy tortillas that you can make right at home. You'll save precious time and energy with the easy-to-use Victoria Cast Iron tortilla press. All while producing the most perfect, fresh tortillas. Not only will you learn how to press the perfect tortilla, you'll also get 101 amazing, delicious recipes to try out with your killer corn tortillas. Did we mention you can make more than just tortillas with these totally tasty recipes? That's right. Meals bursting with home-cooked flavor like chilaquiles, quesadillas, pizza—even French toast!

Turn Tasty Tortillas into Delicious Meals with 101 Recipes

No matter what your favorite meal, the Victoria Cast Iron tortilla press is great for whipping up something for every meal of the day, including snacks. You can explore the world of Mexican cuisine and make mouthwatering enchiladas, quesadillas, taquitos, and chilaquiles. Of course, that's not all! Our 101 recipes also go outside the foodie box. Think—sweet French toast for breakfast, tantalizing queso fundido that will turn into your favorite party dip, nourishing wrap sandwiches for lunch, spicy ancho chicken soup on days you need a dinner to warm up—even tortilla s'mores for family dessert fun! The possibilities of cooking up quick and easy meals with your Victoria Cast Iron tortilla press are endless. Especially with all of the tantalizing recipes you get in this book!

A Whole New World of Deliciously Healthy, Natural Recipes!

When it comes to eating healthy, clean, and natural, the Victoria Cast Iron tortilla press will introduce you to a beautiful world of fresh homemade food that tastes like restaurant-quality, wholesome food. Filling, delicious, and full of fiber, corn tortillas are a great way to add carbohydrates and fiber to your diet while cutting out wheat. Since the tortillas are made right in the comfort of your own home, you know exactly what ingredients are in them. If you're following a paleo, gluten free, dairy free, or vegan lifestyle, the Victoria Cast Iron tortilla press is one way to make killer, unique meals all while sticking to your healthy lifestyle—no matter which healthful way you choose to live.

Achieve Health Goals in Super-Tasty Scrumptious Ways!

When it comes to changing up your diet to meet a more healthy lifestyle, this is the way to go! You can add vegetables, fruit, non-complex carbs, and so much more in just a pinch. This truly is one amazing way to promote more healthy eating choices for yourself or the whole family. Using the Victoria Cast Iron tortilla press, you'll get the opportunity to start making more health conscious choices with the 101 zestful recipes that will have your taste buds doing back flips. Trade complex carbs that can be difficult to digest for corn tortillas and watch the pounds melt off when you combine your healthy eating with a sweet balance of moderate physical fitness.

Learn Insider Tips to Get the Most Out of Your
Victoria Cast Iron Tortilla Press

Not only will you get 101 recipes to try with your Victoria Cast Iron tortilla press, you'll learn just how to get the most out of your tortilla press every time you use it! You'll also learn just how to prep your masa for the best, perfectly round, thin tortillas you have ever made—or eaten for the matter! Plus, other little ways to make your experience with the Victoria Cast Iron tortilla press the best it can possibly be. You'll learn the best ways to prep, store, and condition your tortilla press for continuous, easy use. You'll also speed up your tortilla making process so you can whip up delicious meals in no time for the whole family.

2

Why Choose the Victoria Cast Iron Tortilla Press?

The Most Amazing, Easy to Use One-Press Tortilla Maker Out There!

The Victoria Cast Iron tortilla press is hand casted in Colombia. The best part about this tortilla press is that assembly is quick and to the point. It also comes pre-seasoned with Kosher single source Colombian palm oil, so there's no need to go through any type of pre-maintenance hassle. The weight of the cast iron does all the work. You just add your masa, press, relax and moments later—perfect, thin tortillas for cooking up your favorite recipe from the tantalizing 101 recipes included below.

Stick to The Latest Clean Eating, Paleo, Non-dairy, and Gluten Free Trends

If you're trying to adhere to a strict diet with modifications, the Victoria Cast Iron tortilla press can help you do it with extreme ease. No more wondering if your tortillas really are paleo, non-dairy, or gluten free. No more timely effort pressing your own tortillas by kneading dough a million times just to perfectly hand rolling them. You can implement clean eating in just a few simple steps using the aid of the amazing Victoria Cast Iron tortilla press. It truly is one handy appliance to help you go clean and healthy. This is great for those trying to limit their wheat intake as well because it's great meal replacement for bread—just use delicious tortillas instead!

Toss Out Preservatives, GMOs and Pesticides for a Healthier Diet

Are you on the road to being more health conscious by implementing cool tools and foods to help you toss out preservatives, GMOs and pesticides for a more clean diet? Then the Victoria Cast Iron tortilla press is just the thing for you. You can add super fun recipes to meal time, new foods you've never tried, tantalizing ingredients to spice up your life and so much more, all with the aid of one fun kitchen appliance that makes clean cooking way more quick and easy. You choose all of the ingredients that go into your tortillas and new found recipes, so you'll know they came with your own clean stamp of approval in lieu of store-bought items you just aren't sure about! The best part about going clean and non-GMO, you can grow your own corn or buy from local farmers' markets in order to make fresh masa right at home.

The Best Way to Say Goodbye to Hand-Rolling!

Hand rolling is super time-consuming and can be hard for some people to knead the dough as much as needed. Some people simply don't have the ability to roll their own tortillas. From ailments to age, you don't have to give up those scrumptious homemade corn tortillas just because you can't knead masa or hand roll. The Victoria Cast Iron tortilla press is so simple and easy to use; the whole family will want to get in on all the foodie fun. The Victoria Cast Iron tortilla press does all the hard hand work for you. With 101 recipes to choose from, you might find some new family favorites too!

Helps You Introduce Healthy Treats and Snacks to Kids!

Kids can be picky when it comes to food but not when you introduce them to the Victoria Cast Iron tortilla press. Not only it is a great opportunity to teach kids about how to get around the kitchen in a safe but fun way, it's also a great way to sneak healthy food right into their favorite style snacks and treats. With the 101 recipes included, you'll surely find something sweet and savory to add to the list of fun foods for kids. Use your Victoria Cast Iron tortilla press when school is out for rainy day, snow day, or summer activities to give kids something super fun to do while they learn about healthy food.

For More Than Just Tortillas!

While you'll likely be using your tortilla press for your favorite tortilla recipes, you can also use it to make things like pizza dough! Not to mention flatbread, nacho chips, tacos, migas, burritos, enchiladas, turnovers, tostadas, and more. You can use your Victoria Cast Iron tortilla press to make just about any kind of base or substitute dough you want. Even pies! The possibilities are endless, especially with all the scrumptious recipes you get in this book!

3

A Brief History of the Tortilla

The Bread of Mexico

The word tortilla comes from the Spanish word "torta" which means round cake. The tortilla got its name from Spanish conquerors who landed on Mexico in search for gold. The tortilla was born from the main diet of the Mayans and Aztecs being corn. The Tortilla Industry Association's account on the history of the tortilla is quite fascinating,

"According to Mayan legend, tortillas were invented by a peasant for his hungry king in ancient times. The first tortillas, which date approximately 10,000 years before Christ, were made of native corn with dried kernel. Today, corn tortillas are made from either corn cooked in a lime-based solution or by using corn flour, producing a dough, forming it like a pancake and finally baking it in an oven. Among native Mexicans, tortillas are also commonly used as eating utensils. In the Old West, "cowpokes" realized the versatility of tortillas and used tortillas filled with meat or other foods as a convenient way to eat around the campfire."

In ancient times, the tortilla was made by grinding dried corn kernels into meal on a slab of stone which was then turned into corn dough, or masa, and patted out by hand. Today's tortillas are still prepared using the same ingredients, but which method of making them is better—hand rolling or the tortilla press?

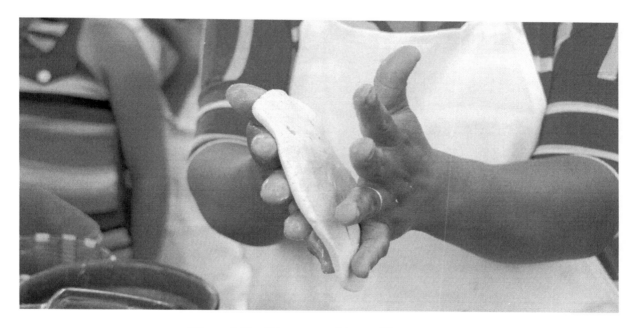

Hand Rolling vs. Tortilla Press

There is only one distinct difference in hand rolling a tortilla and using a tortilla press, and that is simply: kneading the dough. When you make hand tortillas from scratch you will have to knead the dough several times to get it flat or thin enough for frying or baking. If you choose to use the Victoria Cast Iron Tortilla Press, the weight of the cast iron does that for you. All you have to do is roll your masa into a ball, stick it right on the press and lower the handle. Hand rolling is very time consuming, and while preferred, can be tedious in lieu of the quick easy hand press. The Victoria Cast Iron tortilla press gives you perfect tortillas in just 15 seconds or less!

	CORN TORTILLA	FLOUR TORTILLA
CALORIES	40	110
Total Fat (g)	0.5	2.5
Carbs (g)	8	18
Fiber (g)	1	1
Sugar (g)	1	1
Protein(g)	1	3
Sodium(g)	5	320

The Great Tortilla Recipe Debate

Quite often you may hear people argue which tortilla is better: Flour or Corn? Corn has seen a major trend when it comes to adding healthy carbs to your diet. These days it seems to rank much higher with foodies who love eating clean or non-complex carbohydrates with their healthy diet. No matter which you prefer, corn tortillas are a traditional food made from recipes dating back to the Mayans, and have been a staple in authentic Mexican cuisine for many years. Using the Victoria Cast Iron tortilla press to make corn tortillas is a great way to add healthy meals to your diet without sacrificing taste or flavor.

Still can't decide? Have a look for yourself. Here is a nutritional comparison of Mission's yellow corn tortilla and flour tortilla.

Looks like the corn tortilla is the healthier way to go!

Make Your Own Tortillas Instead of Buying Them

Making your own tortillas is a great way to cut down on food costs, as well as time spent in the kitchen preparing elaborate meals. You still get tantalizing taste explosion with tortillas as the base of your favorite meals, snacks, and desserts. The quick and easy 101 recipes will help you add amazing dishes to your weekly eats, and eat super healthy too! Fresh made tortillas are so scrumptious, and you'll know exactly what you are putting in your body with our delicious, simple masa recipe. You'll start spending more time picking out scrumptious new ingredients to whip up killer new recipes and less time in the grocery store deciding what to eat.

Cast Iron over Aluminum: Why Victoria Cast Iron Tortilla Press is the Best Way to Whip up the Healthiest Tortillas!

Cast iron over aluminum is often one of the most common questions to come up when buying a tortilla press. Simply put: The Victoria Cast Iron Tortilla Press is the best way to whip up delicious, healthy tortillas because of the weight of the cast iron, and how quick and easy it is to use. The weight continually presses without any effort on your end, so your tortillas come out thin and perfect in lieu of the thick tortillas that can be harder to use for burritos and wraps and take longer to cook than cast iron pressed tortillas. Not to mention the fact that with cast-iron there's no harsh chemicals or soap with by product to use when cleaning. You just use natural, hot water. So, you'll be spending less overall and being more conscious about what you are putting in your amazing body.

4

Basic Operations

Preparing Your Victoria Cast Iron Tortilla Press for The First Use

Remove the Victoria Cast Iron tortillas press from the box. Set aside the pressing arm and screw. Thoroughly rinse the top and base in hot water before the first use. As the cast iron is pre-seasoned do not use soap or any type of harsh chemical based cleaner on your Victoria Cast Iron tortilla press. Be sure to dry your Victoria Cast Iron tortilla press thoroughly before you assemble it!

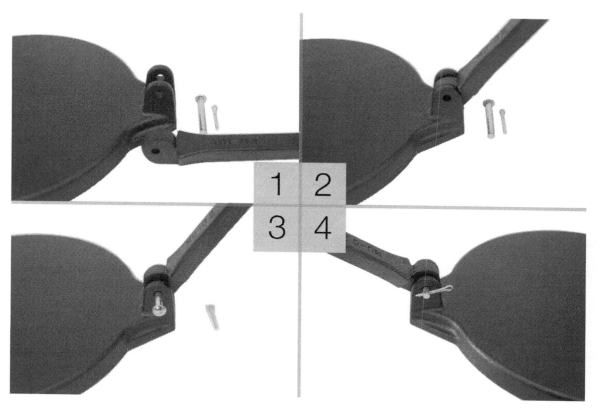

How to Assemble Your Victoria Cast Iron Tortilla Press

1.   Place the top of the tortilla press on top of the base.

2. Place the arm in the slot of the base, and align the rivet (holes) of the arm with the holes of the base.

3. Slide the screw/pin through the aligned holes to secure the handle in place. As this may be difficult to get all the way in, use a hammer to make sure the pin is securely in place.

4. The arm should move with ease and press the top to the base. Now, you are ready to make your first tortillas!

How to Maintain and Store Your Victoria Cast Iron Tortilla Press

Immediately place the Victoria Cast Iron tortilla press in hot water after use. Use a brush to remove any food debris. Again, do not use soap or cleaner on your tortilla press; this will ruin the seasoning. Rinse the press and dry thoroughly. Before storing, rub the tortilla press with vegetable shortening, palm oil or shortening spray. Wipe clean with a paper towel. Store your Victoria Cast Iron tortilla press in a cool, dry place away from harsh elements like the sun.

5

How To Use Your Victoria Tortilla Press Like an Expert

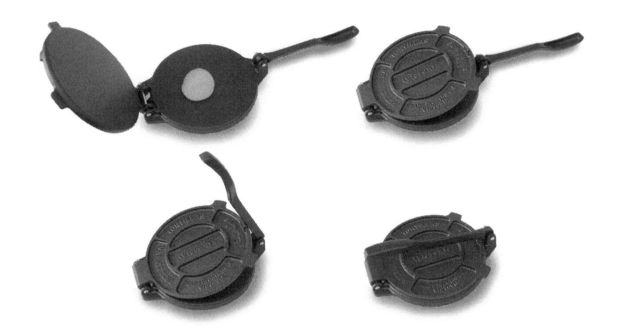

Work with The Right Amount of Dough

Weigh out 2-ounce portions of masa. Each will make one tortilla. This will be roughly the size of a large egg. If you find that your dough is pressing outside of the tortilla press, resize each ball to be the size of a medium egg. Working with the right amount of dough is a process you might have to work out with a few tries seeing that recipes can be different in consistency of dough/masa.

How to Make Perfectly Flat & Round, Delicious Tortillas

Open your tortilla press. Place a small dough ball of masa onto the base, slightly off-center, toward the arm of the press. This area presses the dough first and will keep it from going over the edges—creating a more even, round tortilla. Lower the arm of the press closing the top onto the base, and press using minimal effort. Lift the arm and remove the tortilla.

The Best Tool to Use to Keep Tortillas from Sticking to One Another

In lieu of parchment paper, plastic wrap or wax paper, try using a heavy duty sheet of plastic. Get yourself a quality plastic baggy with a zip-closure that you would normally use for storing food in the freezer. Cut zipper off in a clean line. Next cut open the plastic bag, following the natural lines, and separate it into two pieces. Place one sheet under the masa ball and one sheet on top. Then proceed to press and stack your pressed tortillas.

How to Get Those Amazing Thin Tortillas

Want to get amazingly thin, restaurant-quality tortillas every time you press? You'll need to press one ball individually. Then lay it on wax paper, parchment paper or plastic. Layer a second piece of paper or plastic on top. Press and second ball, and so on. Once you have three stacked together, separated by paper or plastic, press the stack all together. Next, open the tortilla press and flip the tortilla stack, then press again. Open the press a third time and place the middle tortilla on the bottom, and press. In 15 seconds, you'll have three perfectly thin tortillas.

The Best Method for Transferring Dough to Press

After pressing one tortilla with the Victoria Cast Iron, simply lift the top plastic sheet off of the tortilla. Next, pick up the bottom plastic sheet and turn the tortilla over onto the palm of your hand. Gravity will help you peel the second sheet off of the pressed tortilla dough very easy and won't damage the tortilla itself. Then simply place the tortilla onto a heated griddle and cook it to perfection using one of the sweet 101 recipes below!

6

Basic Corn and Flour Tortillas

Fresh Homemade Corn Tortillas

Servings: 20 | Prep Time: 35 minutes | Cook Time: 30 minutes

When it comes to making your own corn tortillas from scratch, have no fear. It's super easy and very healthy—especially when you enlist the help of your Victoria Cast Iron tortilla press. Whip up fresh corn tortillas stuffed with your favorite ingredients or try one of the sweet recipes below to indulge in this scrumptious recipe.

Ingredients:

2 cups masa harina

1 1/2 teaspoons sea salt

1 1/2 cups hot water

Sheet of plastic ziploc bag (cut in half)

Instructions:

5. Mix the masa harina and sea salt together in a large mixing bowl. Slowly pour in the water, stirring to combine.

6. Knead the dough for one minute with your hands until it is smooth, no longer sticky, and can be easily rolled into a small ball. If the dough is crumbly or still sticky, add 1 teaspoon of water and knead until it reaches the smooth consistency. If the dough is too wet add a 1/4 teaspoon of masa harina until smooth.

7. Leave the dough ball in the bowl and cover with a towel.

8. Set it aside and let the dough rest for 15 to 30 minutes in a cool, dry space.

9. Roll the dough into individual balls the size of a medium egg by pinching off a tablespoons of dough. One dough ball makes one 6-inch tortilla.

10. Open the Victoria Cast Iron tortilla press and lay a piece of plastic down. Place a dough ball near the back middle of the bottom plate.

11. Place a second piece of plastic on top of the ball.

12. Pull the arm down in order to press the dough with the tortilla press. If the tortilla isn't thin enough or as even as you would prefer, rotate the tortilla in the plastic and re-press.

13. Open the press and peel the top plastic off the tortilla first. Flip the tortilla over onto your palm and peel the back piece of plastic off the tortilla.

14. Continue pressing tortillas until you use all of the dough.

15. Pre-heat a cast iron griddle or large cast iron skillet over medium-high heat.

16. Gently lay in each tortilla so that they are not overlapping. Cook each tortilla for 1 to 2 minutes until the edges start to curl up. Flip and cook on the other side for 1 to 2 minutes. When the bottoms look dry and pebbly, both sides should be dry to the touch and slightly browned in places.

17. Place the cooked tortillas in a towel, wrap to steam while you are cooking the rest of the tortillas.

18. Stuff and serve with your favorite ingredients, or cool and refrigerate your homemade tortillas for up to 3 days.

Nutritional Info: Calories: 42, Sodium: 142 mg, Dietary Fiber: 1.1 g, Total Fat: 0.4 g, Total Carbs: 8.7 g, Protein: 1.1 g.

Fresh Homemade Flour Tortillas

Servings: 15 | Prep Time: 15 minutes | Cook Time: 10 minutes

The Victoria Cast Iron tortilla press isn't just for masa harina recipes or corn tortillas. Sometimes fluffy flour tortillas just hit the spot when making delicious, gooey burritos, quesadillas or Mexican pies! When you are sincerely craving homemade fluffy tortillas, this is the recipe for you!

Ingredients:

3 1/2 cups all-purpose flour

3 tablespoons vegetable shortening, chilled

1 teaspoon sea salt

2 teaspoons baking powder

1 1/2 cups water

Instructions:

1. Combine flour, salt, baking powder in a large mixing bowl.
2. Fold in vegetable shortening using your hands. Break up the shortening until it is completely incorporated into the dry mix and has slightly crumbly texture.
3. Pour 2/3 cups of water into the mixing bowl and hand knead it into the dough.
4. Add water by one tablespoon at a time, while continuing to knead the dough until you have a smooth dough, that is not sticky or tacky to the touch.
5. Roll the dough into small balls the size of a medium egg.
6. Open the Victoria Tortilla Press and lay a piece of plastic or parchment paper onto the base.
7. Place one dough ball in the press.
8. Place a second piece of plastic or parchment paper on top and lower the arm of the press.
9. Press the dough for 15 seconds.

10. Remove the tortilla from the press and peel the paper or plastic off. Set aside, and continue to press until all dough balls are used.

11. Pre-heat a large cast iron skillet or frying pan over high heat.

12. Place the tortillas in the pan; make sure they are not overlapping.

13. Cook each tortilla for 1 minute on each side until slightly browned.

14. Stuff with your favorite ingredients and serve immediately.

15. Store leftover tortillas in the refrigerator for up to three days.

Nutritional Info: Calories: 129, Sodium: 127 mg, Dietary Fiber: 0.8 g, Total Fat: 2.9 g, Total Carbs: 22.6 g, Protein: 3.0 g.

7

Appetizers

Ancho Chicken Tortilla Soup

Servings: 4-6 | Prep Time: 10 minutes | Cook Time: 15 minutes

Warm things up with some sincerely delicious and tantalizing Ancho Chicken Tortilla Soup. Ancho chilies are the perfect pepper to add warmth instead of heat when it comes to spicing things up a bit. Top with crunchy, fresh homemade tortilla crisps for endless foodie fun.

Ingredients:

4 corn tortillas, made using Victoria Cast Iron tortilla press

Cooking spray

2 large ancho chilies, chopped

2 cups chicken stock

2 tablespoons olive oil

2 cups frozen corn kernels, defrosted

1 large onion, chopped

1 poblano pepper, seeded and chopped

2 cloves garlic, finely chopped

1 teaspoon ground cumin

1 1/2 teaspoon smoked sweet paprika

1/2 teaspoon ground cinnamon

1 (28-ounce) can crushed tomatoes

1 teaspoon honey

1 rotisserie chicken, skinned and shredded

1 teaspoon salt

1 teaspoon fresh ground black pepper

2-4 cups water

1 lime, juiced and zested

Sour cream, for garnish

Cilantro, for garnish

Corn Tortillas:

1/2 cup masa harina

1/2 teaspoon sea salt

1/2 cup hot water

Sheet of plastic ziploc bag (cut in half)

[please see page 29 for instructions]

Instructions:

1. Heat the oven to 350 degrees Fahrenheit. Slice the tortillas into thin strips and scatter on large baking sheet. Spray with cooking spray and bake until golden and crisp. Remove from the oven and set aside.

2. Add the ancho chilies and the chicken stock to a soup pot and bring to a boil over medium heat. Reduce heat to low and simmer until the chilies are tender. Remove from the heat to cool.

3. Heat a medium soup pot with olive oil over high heat. Add the corn and sauté for 2-3 minutes, until charred at the edges. Reduce the heat to medium-high. Add the onions, poblano pepper and garlic. Season with cumin, smoked paprika and cinnamon. Sauté for 5 minutes. Then stir in the tomatoes.

4. Puree the ancho chili stock in a food processor or blender. Fold it to the soup pot. Stir in the honey, shredded chicken, salt and pepper. Add 2 to 4 cups of water to thin soup and simmer over low heat for 5 minutes.

5. Add juice and zest of one lime to the soup.

6. Ladle soup into bowls. Top with some crispy tortilla strips, sour cream and a little cilantro.

Nutritional Info: Calories: 248 | Sodium: 650 mg | Dietary Fiber 8.5 g | Total Fat: 6.3 g | Total Carbs: 39.6 g | Protein: 12.8 g.

Asparagus Cigars

Servings: 28 | Prep Time: 10 minutes | Cook Time: 30 minutes

Sometimes you have to think outside the box when it comes to snacking or party food. That's why these Asparagus Cigars are a great way to get the party started! Simple, easy and super quick to whip up—this recipe will have you wanting to use your tortilla press more often.

Ingredients:

1-pound asparagus

12 flour tortillas, made using Victoria Cast Iron tortilla press

1 large egg

1 pinch salt

2 tablespoons sesame seeds

1 cup olive oil

2 tablespoons soy sauce

2 tablespoons fresh lime juice

2 tablespoons water

1/2 teaspoon sugar substitute

1 scallion, finely chopped

Flour Tortillas:

3 1/2 cups all-purpose flour

3 tablespoons vegetable shortening, chilled

1 teaspoon sea salt

2 teaspoons baking powder

1 1/2 cups water

[please see page 31 for instructions]

Instructions

1. Combine soy sauce, lime juice, water, sugar substitute and scallion in a small mixing bowl. Stir until sugar substitute dissolves. Set aside for dipping.

2. Trim ends of the asparagus to make 6 inch sticks.

3. Crack egg into a mixing bowl, and beat with pinch of salt.

4.   Cut tortillas in half. Brush one half of a tortilla with egg mix and place 1-piece asparagus along the cut side. Tightly roll up tortilla. Insert a toothpick crosswise to secure. Brush the outside of roll with egg mix and sprinkle with sesame seeds; repeat for the rest of the asparagus.

5.   Pour one half inch of olive oil into a 10 inch, heavy duty, frying pan. Heat on medium-high heat until oil crackles when cold water is sprinkled into it.

6.   Add three cigars to the oil and fry, turning once, for three to five minutes or until golden brown. Transfer finish cigars to a paper towel lined plate.

7.   Serve with sweet soy sauce dip.

Nutritional Info: Calories: 95 | Sodium: 76 mg | Dietary Fiber: 1.1 g | Total Fat: 8.0 g | Total Carbs: 5.7 g | Protein: 1.4 g.

Baja Style Fish Tacos

Servings: 4 | Prep Time: 5 minutes | Cook Time: 15 minutes

"Surf's up" when it comes to these tantalizing tacos! If you love restaurant style quality fish tacos Baja style, get ready to make them right at home. Fresh tortillas made right in your Victoria Cast Iron Tortilla Press make all the difference. Serve these bad boys up with a Mexican cerveza and just take it all in.

Ingredients:

For the Cream Sauce:

1/4 cup mayonnaise

2/3 cups sour cream

1 teaspoon grated lemon zest

2 tablespoons fresh lemon juice

2 tablespoons water

Salt and freshly ground black pepper

For the Beer Batter:

1 cup flour

1 teaspoon salt

1/2 teaspoon ground black pepper

1 bottle dark beer, like Dosequis

For the Fish:

2/3 cups olive oil

1 cup flour

1 teaspoon salt

1 teaspoon coarse black pepper

1-pound cod, cut into 1-inch-thick pieces

8 corn tortillas, made using Victoria Cast Iron tortilla press

2 cups cabbage, thinly sliced

2 cups salsa verde, for garnish

Pickled jalapenos, for garnish

8 lime wedges, for garnish

Corn Tortillas:

1 cup masa harina

1 teaspoon sea salt

1 cup hot water

Sheet of plastic ziploc bag (cut in half)

[please see page 29 for instructions]

Instructions:

1. Combine the mayonnaise and sour cream in a large mixing bowl. Fold in the lemon zest, lemon juice and water. Season with salt and pepper.

2. Mix the flour, salt and pepper in a separate mixing bowl. Gradually add in the beer while whisking. Set aside and let the batter rest for 15 minutes.

3. Add 1/3 cup olive oil to a deep-frying pan over medium heat. Heat the oil until water crackles when sprinkled into oil.

4. On a large plate, combine the flour and salt. Season the fish pieces all over with salt and pepper and coat with the flour.

5. Dip the floured fillets in the beer batter and coat on both sides. Transfer to the hot oil and fry until golden brown—about 5 minutes each.

6. Transfer fish to paper towel lined plate to drain.

7. Assemble the tacos by laying two tortillas on a plate. Lay two to three pieces of fish in the middle. Top fish with cream, shredded cabbage, salsa verde and pickled jalapenos.

Nutritional Info: Calories: 928 | Sodium: 247 mg | Dietary Fiber: 5.8 g | Total Fat: 49.6 g | Total Carbs: 80.1 g | Protein: 37.4 g.

Bean Enchiladas

Servings: 5 | Prep Time: 10 minutes | Cook Time: 30 minutes

Vegetarian comfort food is just as easy with the Victoria Cast Iron Tortilla Press. Turn your tortillas in to creamy, cheesy treats topped with scrumptious enchilada sauce. Simple and easy, serve them up with roasted vegetables for a healthy meal.

Ingredients:

10 corn tortillas, made using Victoria Cast Iron tortilla press

1 (15-ounce) can refried beans

1 tablespoon olive oil

1 onion, chopped

1 (4-ounce) can ancho chilies in adobo sauce, chopped

1 (15-ounce) can crushed tomatoes

1 teaspoon chili powder

1 teaspoon cumin powder

1 teaspoon garlic powder

1 teaspoon sea salt

1 teaspoon black pepper

1 vegetable bouillon cube, dissolved in 1 tablespoon hot water

4 cups oaxaca cheese, grated

Corn Tortillas:

1 cup masa harina

1 teaspoon sea salt

1 cup hot water

Sheet of plastic ziploc bag (cut in half)

[please see page 29 for instructions]

Instructions:

1. Heat the oil in a large frying pan on medium heat. Cook the onions for 5-8 minutes until soft. Sprinkle in the chili powder, cumin, garlic salt and pepper. Cook for 1 minute more.

2. Pour in the tomatoes and ancho chilies. Turn heat up to medium-high and bring to a boil. Fold in the dissolved vegetable bouillon cube. Turn down the heat and simmer for 5-10 minutes, stirring occasionally, until thickened.

3. Pre-heat oven to 350 degrees Fahrenheit. Spread 1/4 of the sauce onto the bottom of a baking dish.

4. Spread a spoonful of the beans down the middle of each tortilla. Top beans with cheese. Roll up and place seam side down in the baking dish. Repeat until all enchiladas are rolled.

5. Pour remaining sauce on top. Top with remaining cheese. Bake for 25-30 minutes or cheese is bubbly.

Nutritional Info: Calories: 298 | Sodium: 1173 mg | Dietary Fiber 13.1 g | Total Fat: 6.6 g | Total Carbs: 50.7 g | Protein: 11.9 g.

Black Bean and Mango Tostadas

Servings: 4 | Prep Time: 10 minutes | Cook Time: 5 minutes

Cool, creamy and just a hint of sweet make these black bean mango tostadas absolutely to die for! Super quick and easy, they'll surely become one of your favorite recipes to go along with fresh tortillas made with your Victoria Cast Iron tortilla press. Cut them into triangles and serve them as bite size tostadas for endless party fun!

Ingredients

1 (15-ounce) can black beans, rinsed and drained

1 tablespoon olive oil

2 scallions, finely chopped

1/2 teaspoon chili powder

1/4 teaspoon sea salt

4 flour tortillas, made using Victoria Cast Iron tortilla press

1 cup monterey jack cheese, shredded

1 ripe mango, peeled, pitted and diced

2 tablespoons red onion, finely chopped

1 tablespoon cilantro, finely chopped

1 tablespoon lime juice

1/2 teaspoon lime zest

Cooking spray, like coconut or olive oil spray

Flour Tortillas:

1 cup all-purpose flour

3 teaspoons vegetable shortening, chilled

1/4 teaspoon sea salt

1/2 teaspoon baking powder

1/2 cup water

Sheet of plastic ziploc bag (cut in half)

[please see page 31 for instructions]

Instructions

1. Pre-heat oven to 425 degrees Fahrenheit. Combine black beans, olive oil, scallions, chili powder and sea salt in a large mixing bowl.

2. Coat a baking sheet with a layer of cooking spray. Place tortillas on baking sheet and spoon bean mixture on top. Add an even layer of cheese.

3. Bake 10 minutes; until golden and crisp, about

4. Combine mango, onion, cilantro, lime juice and zest in a small mixing bowl.

5. Remove tostadas from oven. Top with mango salsa and serve.

Nutritional Info: Calories: 561 | Sodium: 290 mg | Dietary Fiber: 18.3 g | Total Fat: 14.3 g | Total Carbs: 79.6 g | Protein: 31.5 g.

Cannelloni (or Italian Enchiladas)

Servings: 6 | Prep Time: 10 minutes | Cook Time: 40 minutes

Tortillas don't always mean Mexican when it comes to delicious flavor. Go for a taste of Italy when it comes to using your Victoria Cast Iron Tortilla Press. Serve it up family style with bruschetta, a big garden salad and espresso or limoncello for dessert with biscotti.

Ingredients:

1 tablespoon olive oil

3 garlic cloves, minced

1 teaspoon dried oregano

1/2 teaspoon sea salt

1/2-pound ground veal or beef

1/2 (14-ounce) can artichoke hearts, drained and roughly chopped

1 cup baby spinach, chopped

1 cup ricotta cheese

2 large egg yolks

1/4 cup chopped fresh basil leaves

3 cups marinara sauce

1/4 cup red wine

10 corn tortillas, warmed, made using Victoria Cast Iron tortilla press

2 cups mozzarella cheese, shredded

1/2 cup parmesan cheese, grated for garnish

Corn Tortillas:

1 cup masa harina

1 teaspoon sea salt

1 cup hot water

Sheet of plastic ziploc bag (cut in half)

[please see page 29 for instructions]

Instructions:

1.   Preheat oven to 350 degrees Fahrenheit.

2. Add ricotta and egg yolks to a small mixing bowl and whisk until it forms a thick cream.

3. Heat oil in large skillet over medium-high heat. Add garlic and oregano. Cook 1 minute, stirring constantly.

4. Add veal and salt. Cook 8 minutes or until browned; break up the meat with a wooden spoon or spatula as it cooks.

5. Remove skillet from heat. Stir in artichokes, spinach and basil. Fold ricotta mix into the skillet and stir until well blended.

6. Spread 1 cup marinara sauce in the bottom of an 11x14-inch glass baking dish. Place corn tortillas flat on a work surface. Spoon one 1/2 cup meat mixture down the center of a tortilla. Roll it up and place seam side down in the baking dish; repeat with remaining tortillas. Top enchiladas with remaining marinara sauce; sprinkle with mozzarella cheese.

7. Bake for 29 minutes. Garnish with Parmesan cheese and serve.

Nutritional Info: Calories: 491 | Sodium: 1035 mg | Dietary Fiber: 7.8 g | Total Fat: 21.2 g | Total Carbs: 43.3 g | Protein: 31.4 g.

Chicken Salad with Crispy Tortillas

Servings: 4 | Prep Time: 10 minutes | Cook Time: 10 minutes

Give this sweet and savory Chicken Salad some seriously tasty depth with crispy homemade tortillas! Everyone loves a good chicken salad, so why not make one that hits the spot. This quick and easy salad can be prepped the night before for one killer lunch. Just be sure to take your tortilla crisps in a separate container!

Ingredients:

3/4 cups olive oil

6 corn tortillas, cut into 1/2-inch strips, made using Victoria Cast Iron tortilla press

1/2 teaspoon sea salt

1 small head romaine lettuce, chopped

3 cups rotisserie chicken, shredded

1 carrot, shredded

4 radishes, sliced

For Salad Dressing:

2 teaspoons balsamic vinegar

1 teaspoon lemon juice

2 teaspoons olive oil

1/2 teaspoon sugar substitute

1/2 teaspoon Italian seasoning

1/2 teaspoon garlic powder

Coarse ground black pepper, for garnish

Corn Tortillas:

Sheet of plastic ziploc bag (cut in half)

2 cups masa harina

[please see page 29 for instructions]

1/2 tablespoon sea salt

1 1/2 cups hot water

Instructions:

1. Heat 3/4 cups olive oil in a large frying pan on medium-high heat. Fry the tortilla strips for 3 to 4 minutes, tossing frequently, until crisp.

2. Transfer tortilla chips to a paper towel lined plate and season with sea salt.

3. Add salad dressing ingredient to a large mixing bowl and stir until sugar substitute is dissolved.

4. Add the lettuce, chicken, carrot, and radishes to the vinaigrette and toss well to coat.

5. Dish salad out onto individual plates and top with tortilla crisps.

Nutritional Info: Calories: 635 | Sodium: 882 mg | Dietary Fiber: 3.3 g | Total Fat: 42.7 g | Total Carbs: 24.5 g | Protein: 44.0 g.

Chicken Tortilla Soup

Servings: 4 | Prep Time: 10 minutes | Cook Time: 25 minutes

Get warm and cozy up to a hearty bowl of healthy Chicken Tortilla Soup. This recipe is sure to send your taste buds into a tantalizing explosion with its roasted veggies and kick of Cayenne! Enjoy this with your favorite cerveza with a wedge of lime or a fresh garden salad on the side.

Ingredients

1 cup rapeseed oil

1/2 cup elbow pasta

2 tablespoons olive oil

2 cloves garlic, minced

1 onion, diced

4 cups chicken stock

1 (28-ounce) can crushed tomatoes

1 (4-ounce) can green chilies

2 teaspoons chili powder

1 1/2 teaspoons cumin

1/2 teaspoon oregano

Pinch of cayenne pepper

1/4 teaspoon kosher salt

1/4 teaspoon fresh ground black pepper

2 cups chicken breast, cooked and shredded

1 cup corn kernels, roasted

2 tablespoons cilantro, chopped

1 lime juices

1 avocado, diced

5 corn tortillas, made using Victoria Cast Iron tortilla press

Corn Tortillas:

[please see page 29 for instructions]

1/2 cup masa harina

1/2 teaspoon sea salt

Sheet of plastic ziploc bag (cut in half)

1/2 cup hot water

Instructions:

1. Add rapeseed oil to a deep saucepan and heat on medium-high. Fry tortilla strips in single layer batches for 1-3 minutes each, until golden crispy. Transfer to a paper towel lined plate to cool. Set aside.

2. In a large pot of boiling salted water, cook pasta per package instructions; drain well. Blanch with cold water.

3. Heat olive oil in a large stockpot or Dutch oven over medium heat. Add garlic and onion, and cook, stirring frequently, until onions have become translucent, about 2-3 minutes.

4. Fold in chicken stock, crushed tomatoes, green chilies, chili powder, cumin, oregano, salt, pepper and cayenne pepper.

5. Cover, reduce to low heat, and simmer until thickened; about 15 minutes.

6. Stir in pasta, chicken, corn, cilantro and lime juice. Cook for 5 minutes.

7. Serve immediately, garnished with fresh tortilla strips and avocado.

Nutritional Info: Calories: 521 | Sodium: 1519 mg | Dietary 11.9 g | Total Fat: 21.4 g | Total Carbs: 51.1 g | Protein: 35.5 g.

Chilaquiles

Servings: 4 | Prep Time: 15 minutes | Cook Time: 15 minutes

Get authentic with your tortilla press and whip up one simple, easy Mexican snack with this delicious recipe. Chilaquiles are known as Mexican comfort food, and not just because it's covered in delicious cheese. Serve this up as an appetizer on Mexican night or enjoy as the perfect afternoon snack.

Ingredients:

3/4 cups and 2 teaspoons olive oil

Sea salt, for sprinkling on tortillas

6 corn tortillas, sliced into small triangles; made using Victoria Cast Iron tortilla press

2/3 cups red enchilada sauce

1/3 cup salsa verde

1/4 cup cotija cheese, crumbled

1/4 small white onion, chopped

1/4 cup fresh cilantro leaves

Corn Tortillas:

2 cups masa harina

1/2 tablespoon sea salt

1 1/2 cups hot water

Sheet of plastic ziploc bag (cut in half)

[please see page 29 for instructions]

Instructions:

1. Heat the olive oil in a large frying pan over medium-high heat. Fry the tortillas for 3 to 4 minutes turning often, until golden and crisp. Sprinkle with sea salt.

2. Drain oil from pan and transfer tortilla chips to a paper towel lined plate.

3. Return the frying pan to the stove and turn to medium heat. Add 2 teaspoons olive oil to pan. Add the enchilada sauce and salsa verde.

4. Add the tortillas chips to the frying pan. Cook for 5 to 10 minutes, turning often, until most of the sauce is absorbed.

5. Top with the cotija, onion, and cilantro. Serve immediately!

Nutritional Info: Calories: 451 | Sodium: 439 mg | Dietary Fiber: 2.7 g | Total Fat: 41.8g | Total Carbs: 19.3 g | Protein: 4.3 g.

Fish Stick Tacos

Servings: 4 | Prep Time: 5 minutes | Cook Time: 15 minutes

For the kids and the kid at heart, welcome to the wild world of fish stick tacos. Nothing beats savory fish sticks, except Fish Stick Tacos! Whip up these delicious treats for an afterschool snack, rainy day lunch, or teach the kids how to cook their favorite meal with one killer Mexican kick.

Ingredients:

1 box frozen fish sticks, breaded

1/2 teaspoon chili powder

3 cups cabbage, shredded

1 cup carrots, shredded

1/4 cup sugar-free mayonnaise

2 tablespoons lime juice

1/4 teaspoon chipotle chili

1/4 teaspoon sea salt

8 corn tortillas, warmed, made using Victoria Cast Iron tortilla press

Fresh salsa, for garnish

Corn Tortillas:

1 cup masa harina

1 teaspoon sea salt

1 cup hot water

Sheet of plastic ziploc bag (cut in half)

[please see page 29 for instructions]

Instructions:

1. Preheat oven to directions on box of fish sticks. Line a baking sheet with aluminum foil. Arrange fish sticks on baking sheet in a single layer. Sprinkle fish sticks with chili powder. Bake according to directions on box.

2. Combine cabbage, carrots, mayonnaise, lime juice, chipotle chili and salt in a medium bowl.

3.   Remove fish sticks and let cool for five minutes. Place two fish sticks per tortilla. Scoop 1 tablespoon slaw on top of each tortilla.

4.   Fold and serve with salsa on the side.

Nutritional Info: Calories: 321 | Sodium: 464 mg | Dietary Fiber: 5.2 g | Total Fat: 13 g | Total Carbs: 42.9 g | Protein: 10.5 g.

Huevos Rancheros in Tortilla Cups

Servings: 4 | Prep Time: 10 minutes | Cook Time: 25 minutes

Huevos Rancheros make for one killer breakfast or brunch item! Why not serve them up on the east side in scrumptious tortilla cups!? This recipe is so easy; the kids will be able to help.

Ingredients:

3 tablespoons olive oil

4 flour tortillas, made using Victoria Cast Iron tortilla press

Sea salt

1 (16-ounce) can refried beans

1 (16-ounce) can black beans, drained and rinsed

1 teaspoon chili powder

1 teaspoon cumin

2 tablespoons cilantro, chopped

4 large eggs

1 cup monterey jack cheese, shredded

1/2 cup fresh salsa

1/4 cup black olives, sliced

1/4 cup avocado, diced

Flour Tortillas:

3 1/2 cups all-purpose flour

3 tablespoons vegetable shortening, chilled

1 teaspoon sea salt

2 teaspoons baking powder

1 1/2 cup water

[please see page 31 for instructions]

Instructions:

1. Preheat the oven to 350 degrees Fahrenheit. Moving one rack to the bottom of the oven.

2. Brush the inner surface of four ramekins with olive oil.

3. Warm the tortillas in a microwave for 10 seconds.

4. Gently press one tortilla into each ramekin; fold the sides over slightly taking care not to tear the tortilla.

5. Use a silicone brush and brush the inside of each tortilla olive oil. Add a pinch of sea salt to each cup.

6. Combine the black beans, cumin, cilantro and one 1/2 tablespoon olive oil in a large mixing bowl.

7. Spread a tablespoon of refried beans into each cup.

8. Spoon about 2/3 cups of the bean mix into each tortilla cup.

9. Carefully crack one egg into the center of each tortilla cup on top of the bean mix.

10. Sprinkle the egg surface with shredded cheese.

11. Place on bottom rack and bake for 25 minutes, or until the whites of each egg are set and no longer runny.

12. Top with salsa, olives and avocado. Serve while piping hot!

Nutritional Info: Calories: 854 | Sodium: 853 mg | Dietary Fiber: 26.4 g | Total Fat: 30.7g | Total Carbs: 103.6 g | Protein: 46.2 g.

Lemon Roasted Chicken Salad Wrap

Servings: 2 | Prep Time: 15 minutes | Cook Time: 2 hours

Here's one super fresh wrap for those who live to eat clean. This tangy taste explosion will soon become a household favorite in no time—especially when you can get more than one meal out of the delicious roast chicken! Consider this recipe "weekly meal planning" at its freshest and finest.

Ingredients:

1 (4-6 pounds) chicken, whole

Olive oil, for coating the chicken

1 teaspoon sea salt

1 teaspoon pepper

2 teaspoons butter

1 shallot, chopped

1 lemon, cut in quarters

1/2 cup sugar-free mayonnaise

2 tablespoons Dijon mustard

2 teaspoons apple cider vinegar

1/2 cup walnuts, chopped

1/4 cup red grapes, chopped

2 celery ribs, chopped

2 lemons, juiced and zested

2 tablespoons tarragon, chopped

1/4 teaspoon sea salt

1/4 teaspoon cracked black pepper

4 leaves romaine lettuce

4 corn tortillas, made using Victoria Cast Iron tortilla press

Corn Tortillas:

1/2 cup masa harina

1/2 teaspoon sea salt

1/2 cup hot water

Sheet of plastic ziploc bag (cut in half)

[please see page 29 for instructions]

Instructions:

1. Pre-heat oven to 350 degrees Fahrenheit and adjust a rack to the lowest position.

2. Place the chicken on a baking sheet or roasting pan lined with aluminum foil.

3. Rub the chicken with olive oil; coat well. Pack the cavity of the chicken with the shallot, butter, lemon, salt and pepper. Place the chicken breast-side down on the pan.

4. Roast the chicken for 30 minutes. Remove from the oven and flip it breast side up. Continue to roast for one more hour. The chicken is done when the leg reads 170 degrees on a meat thermometer or the juices run clear when cut.

5. Cover with aluminum foil and set the chicken aside to rest for 30 minutes.

6. While the chicken is resting, mix the mayonnaise, mustard, walnuts, grapes, celery, onions, lemon juice, lemon zest and tarragon in a large mixing bowl.

7. Uncover the chicken and remove the breasts. Shred the breast meat using a fork.

8. Fold the shredded chicken into the mixing bowl with the lemon dressing.

9. Lay the tortillas flat. Lay one piece of lettuce in the middle of each. Spoon 1/4 to 1/2 cup of lemon roast chicken mix into the lettuce. Fold one side of the tortilla in and roll it up to make a burrito.

10. Refrigerate any leftovers for 1 to 3 days. Use leftover chicken for tortilla soup, casseroles or fajitas!

Nutritional Info: Calories: 1364 | Sodium: 1150 mg | Dietary Fiber: 5.5 g | Total Fat: 44.3 g | Total Carbs: 5.5 g | Protein: 205.1 g.

Moo Shoo Pork

Servings: 6 | Prep Time: 10 minutes | Cook Time: 20 minutes

Craving a little taste of Asia? Moo Shoo Pork is just the thing to wet your appetite. Filled with delicious veggies and lean meat, this is just the thing to hit the sweet and savory spot. Serve it up with a garden salad and ginger dressing for one super-healthy meal.

Ingredients:

3/4-pound boneless pork chops, trimmed and thinly sliced

3 large garlic cloves, minced

2 tablespoons sesame oil

1 teaspoon mirin or rice vinegar

8 scallions, trimmed and sliced

1 cup carrots, shredded

1/2 cup white cabbage, shredded

1/2 cup purple cabbage, shredded

3 tablespoons reduced-sodium soy sauce

4 flour tortillas, made using Victoria Cast Iron tortilla press

For Hoisin Sauce:

4 tablespoons dark soy sauce

2 tablespoons no-sugar added peanut butter

1 tablespoon sugar substitute like Splenda

10 drops hot sauce

1/8 teaspoon black pepper

2 teaspoons mirin or rice vinegar

1/8 teaspoon garlic powder

2 teaspoons sesame oil

Flour Tortillas:

1 cup all-purpose flour

3 teaspoons vegetable shortening, chilled

1/4 teaspoon sea salt

1/2 teaspoon baking powder

1/2 cup water

Sheet of plastic ziploc bag (cut in half)

[please see page 31 for instructions]

Instructions:

1. Pre-heat oven to warm. Wrap tortillas in aluminum foil and place in the oven to warm.

2. Mix all ingredients for Hoisin Sauce together in a mixing bowl. Set aside until needed.

3. Heat 1 tablespoon sesame oil in large wok over medium-high heat. Sauté the pork and half of the garlic for 5 minutes, or until cooked through. Transfer to a mixing bowl.

4. Wipe out the wok with a paper towel.

5. Heat remaining oil in the wok on medium-high. Add scallions, carrots, cabbage and remaining garlic. Cook, stirring occasionally, 8 minutes or until softened. Add 1/2 of the hoisin sauce, mirin and soy sauce. Cook for 2 more minutes.

6. Add the pork; gently heat through, about 2 minutes.

7. Remove tortillas from oven. Brush each tortilla with extra hoisin sauce on one side.

8. Spoon pork mixture down center of each. Roll up like a burrito and serve.

Nutritional Info: Calories: 352 | Sodium: 1022 mg | Dietary 2.8 g | Total Fat: 23.4 g | Total Carbs: 20.3 g | Protein: 16.5 g.

Refried Bean Tostadas

Servings: 5 | Prep Time: 10 minutes | Cook Time: 10 minutes

Sink your teeth into something totally scrumptious when you whip up these healthy, baked Refried Bean Tostadas. Ditch the traditional sandwich when it comes to lunch or afternoon snacks, and go for something more tantalizingly tasty. Quick and simple these are a great starter recipe for little chefs, too!

Ingredients:

3/4 cups refried beans

3/4 cups pico de gallo

1 cup cheddar cheese, shredded

1 tablespoon cilantro, chopped

6 corn tortillas, made using Victoria Cast Iron tortilla press

1 cup romaine lettuce, shredded

2 tablespoons sour cream, for garnish

Corn Tortillas:

1/2 cup masa harina

1/2 teaspoon sea salt

1/2 cup hot water

Sheet of plastic ziploc bag (cut in half)

[please see page 29 for instructions]

Instructions

1. Preheat oven to 400°F. Mist every other cup of a 12-cup muffin tin with nonstick cooking spray. Press a tortilla into each sprayed cup, flattening out edges, and bake until golden, about 8 minutes.

2. Divide beans among tostadas, top with salsa and sprinkle with cheese. Return to oven and bake until warmed through, 7 to 10 minutes.

3. Place each tostada on a plate and sprinkle with cilantro. Top with some lettuce and a small dollop of sour cream. Serve with extra salsa, if desired.

Nutritional Info: Calories: 178 | Sodium: 417 mg | Dietary Fiber: 3.2 g | Total Fat: 8.2 g | Total Carbs: 17.3 g | Protein: 8.0 g.

Smoked Trout & Horseradish Flatbread

Servings: 4 | Prep Time: 10 minutes | Cook Time: 8 minutes

Looking for a new, fun and creative way to liven up your flatbread? Check out this amazing recipe packed with omega 3 rich fish and spicy horseradish for a little kick! Heart healthy and delicious this flatbread is great for lunch, dinner or served as an appetizer shared for two.

Ingredients:

4 flour tortillas, made using Victoria Cast Iron tortilla press

2 tablespoons olive oil, for brushing

2 tablespoons creamed horseradish

2 tablespoons crème fraiche

1 teaspoon dill, chopped

1 teaspoon lemon juice

1/8 teaspoon lemon zest

1/4 teaspoon sea salt

1/4 teaspoon black pepper

1 (3-ounce) can beets, packed in water

4 smoked trout fillets, cut into 1 inch pieces

Flour Tortillas:

3 1/2 cups all-purpose flour

3 tablespoons vegetable shortening, chilled

1 teaspoon sea salt

2 teaspoons baking powder

1 1/2 cup water

[please see page 31 for instructions]

Instructions:

1. Heat oven to 420 degrees Fahrenheit. Brush the tortillas with olive oil. Line a large baking sheet with aluminum foil. Bake tortillas for 8 minutes until golden crisp around the edges.

2. Combine horseradish, crème fraiche, chopped dill, lemon juice and zest, salt and pepper in a mixing bowl.

3. Slice beets thinly and top each flatbread with a few slices and smoked trout.

4. Drizzle with horseradish sauce, sprinkle with dill fronds and serve with a garden salad.

Nutritional Info: Calories: 257 | Sodium: 213 mg | Dietary Fiber 2.3 g | Total Fat: 14.3 g | Total Carbs: 14.2 g | Protein: 18.6 g.

Sour Cream Beef Filled Tortillas

Servings: 6-8 | Prep Time: 10 minutes | Cook Time: 20 minutes

Creamy sour cream filled beef tortillas are super-easy and absolutely delicious! Topped with a simple sauce, these tortillas are especially great for family dinner when you're on the go.

Ingredients:

3 pounds Beef roast, cooked and shredded

2 cups monterey jack cheese, shredded

1 cup sour cream

8 flour tortillas, made using Victoria Cast Iron tortilla press

Flour Tortillas:

2 cups all-purpose flour

4 1/2 teaspoons vegetable shortening, chilled

1/2 teaspoon sea salt

1 teaspoon baking powder

2/3 cups water

Sheet of plastic ziploc bag (cut in half)

[please see page 31 for instructions]

For the Sauce:

1 package of taco seasoning mix

1 (8-ounce) cans of tomato sauce

1/4 cup beef broth

Instructions:

1.	Preheat oven to 400 degrees Fahrenheit.

2.   Combine roast, 1 cup cheese and sour cream in large mixing bowl. Set aside

3.   Combine sauce ingredients and heat in a medium saucepan on medium-heat for 15 minutes.

4.   Spoon mixture onto flour tortillas and roll. Place seam side down in the baking dish. Top with sauce and remaining cheese. Bake 5-10 minutes or until cheese is melted.

Nutritional Info: Calories: 532 | Sodium: 495 mg | Dietary Fiber 1.6 g | Total Fat: 25.8 g | Total Carbs: 11.4 g | Protein: 61.0 g.

Tortilla Soup

Servings: 6-8 | Prep Time: 30 minutes | 55 minutes

Warm things up with the most delicious Tortilla Soup this side of the border! If you love tacos and soup- you will absolutely love this delicious, healthy soup packed with vegetables and protein. Get ready for a taste bud explosion, because this tortilla recipe is sure to knock your socks off!

Ingredients:

8 corn tortillas, quartered and cut into thin strips; made using Victoria Cast Iron tortilla press

1 teaspoon olive oil

3 poblano pepper, chopped and seeded

1 medium onion, chopped

1 pound extra lean ground beef, 15% fat or less like Simple Truth or Laura's Lean Beef

1 (15-ounce) can red kidney beans, drained and rinsed

1 (15-ounce) can lima beans, drained and rinsed

1 (15-ounce) can yellow hominy, drained and rinsed

1 (15-ounce) can pinto beans, drained and rinsed

4 (4-ounce) cans chopped green chilies

3 (15-ounce) stewed tomatoes, chopped

1 package of ranch seasoning mix, like Hidden Valley

1 tablespoon chili powder

1 1/2 teaspoons cumin powder

1/2 teaspoon paprika

1/2 teaspoon sea salt

1/2 teaspoon black pepper

1/4 teaspoon garlic powder

1/4 teaspoon crushed red pepper flakes

1/4 teaspoon dried oregano

2 tablespoons lime juice

4 cups water

2 cups sharp cheddar cheese, shredded

1/4 cup fresh cilantro, chopped

Corn Tortillas:

1 cup masa harina

1 teaspoon sea salt

1 cup hot water

Sheet of plastic ziploc bag (cut in half)

[please see page 29 for instructions]

Instructions:

1. Preheat oven to 400 degrees Fahrenheit.

2. Spread tortilla strips in an even layer on a baking sheet and coat with cooking spray. Bake 12 to 15 minutes until golden crisp. Remove from oven and set aside to cool.

3. Heat oil in a large frying pan on medium heat. Add poblano peppers and onion. Cook for 5 minutes until softened.

4. Add ground beef and cook until browned. Drain and add spices. Cook with spices for one minute until well-blended.

5. Transfer meat mix to a soup pot. Add all the canned ingredients, as well as the tomato juice and water.

6. Bring to a boil, reduce heat and simmer 45 minutes.

7. Remove from the heat and stir in lime juice. Serve each portion topped with tortilla strips, Cheddar cheese and cilantro.

Nutritional Info: Calories: 805 | Sodium: 720 mg | Dietary Fiber: 24.7 g | Total Fat: 16.9 g | Total Carbs: 109.2 g | Protein: 55.6 g.

8

Breakfast Tortillas

Bacon Chard Quesadillas

Servings: 4 | Prep Time: 35 minutes | Cook Time: 35 minutes

This one skillet recipe is so easy; it will soon become a "go to" favorite when it comes to whipping up fresh quesadillas using your Victoria Cast Iron Tortilla Press. Add a super healthy serving of chard to your daily diet. Cooked with warm bacon, these quesadillas simply scream comfort food with a healthy kick.

Ingredients:

4 slices center-cut bacon, chopped

1 small onion, halved and thinly sliced

1 bunch of chard leaves, chopped

1/2 teaspoon freshly ground pepper

1 (15-ounce) can black beans, drained and rinsed

4 flour tortillas, made using Victoria Cast Iron tortilla press

1 cup pepper jack cheese, grated

Coconut oil cooking spray

Flour Tortillas:

1 cup all-purpose flour

3 teaspoons vegetable shortening, chilled

1/4 teaspoon sea salt

1/2 teaspoon baking powder

1/2 cup water

Sheet of plastic ziploc bag (cut in half)

[please see page 31 for instructions]

Instructions:

1. Cook bacon in a large nonstick frying pan on medium-high heat, stirring often, until crisp, 2 to 3 minutes. Drain grease. Return pan to stove. Reduce heat to medium, add onion and cook 2 minutes or until softened.

2.   Add chard and pepper. Cook 1 to 2 minutes until wilted. Add beans and coarsely mash; stir to combine. Remove from heat.

3.   Lay tortillas on a flat work surface. Spread 1/4 cup filling down half of the tortilla. Top with 2 tablespoons cheese. Fold tortillas in half, pressing gently to flatten.

4.   Wipe out the pan with a paper towel and return to medium heat.

5.   Spray with cooking spray. Add 2 quesadillas and cook 2-4 minutes, turning once, until golden on both sides and cheese is melted. Transfer to a platter and tent with aluminum foil to keep warm. Repeat with remaining quesadillas and serve hot!

Nutritional Info: Calories: 750 | Sodium: 819 mg | Dietary Fiber 18.3 g | Total Fat: 28.4 g |
Total Carbs: 79.4 g | Protein: 45.9 g.

Beef and Bean Enchiladas

Servings: 6-8 | Prep Time: 20 minutes | Cook Time: 20 minutes

Melt in your mouth enchiladas stuffed with beef and beans, topped with gooey cheese, is a great way to cook something up that the whole family will enjoy. You can even prep this a day or two in advance with instructions to heat for those days you aren't going to be home in time for dinner!

Ingredients:

Corn Tortillas:

2 cups masa harina

1/2 tablespoon sea salt

1 1/2 cups hot water

Sheet of plastic ziploc bag (cut in half)

[please see page 29 for instructions]

Enchilada Sauce:

3 ancho chilies or poblano peppers

1 teaspoon olive oil

12 tomatillos, husked and quartered

1 medium onion, chopped

2 cloves garlic

1 (10-ounce) can mexican-style diced tomatoes

1 cup beef broth

2 tablespoons cumin

1 tablespoon chili powder

1/2 teaspoon sea salt

1/2 teaspoon ground pepper

Enchilada Filling:

1-pound lean (90% or leaner) ground beef

1 teaspoon chili powder

1/4 teaspoon salt

1 teaspoon garlic powder

1/2 teaspoon oregano

1 (16-ounce) can fat-free refried beans

2 dashes hot sauce

16 corn tortillas, made using Victoria Cast Iron tortilla press

2 cups shredded monterey jack cheese

Instructions

1. Cover a baking sheet with aluminum foil and brush with 1 teaspoon olive oil. Place chilies on the sheet.

2. Set the oven to broil and roast peppers for five minutes. Flip the peppers and roast on the opposite side for five more minutes.

3. Place tomatillos, canned tomatoes, onion, garlic and roast peppers in a food processor or blender on pulse until pureed.

4. Pour into a large saucepan. Add beef broth to the pan. Bring to a simmer over medium-high heat. Reduce heat, cover and cook for 15 minutes; stirring occasionally.

5. Preheat oven to 400 degrees Fahrenheit. Heat a large skillet on medium-high heat. Add ground beef, chili powder, sea salt, garlic powder, and oregano. Cook until completely browned.

6. Add beans and hot sauce to frying pan. Stir to combine. Remove from the heat and set aside.

7. Spread one 1/2 cup of the sauce onto the bottom of a 9 x 13-inch baking dish.

8. Lay the tortillas out on a flat surface. Fill each with 1/4 cup of the beef and bean filling right in the middle of the tortilla. Roll it up into a burrito or taquito shape.

9. Place each tortilla, seam-side down, into the baking dish with each of the enchiladas snugly next to one another to make one single layer.

10. Top the enchiladas with the remaining sauce, then cover with shredded cheese.

11. Bake for 20 minutes until cheese is gooey and melted.

Nutritional Info: Calories: 426 | Sodium: 689 mg | Dietary Fiber: 8.7 g | Total Fat: 16.1 g | Total Carbs: 39.8 g | Protein: 32.4 g.

Breakfast Burrito

Servings: 4 | Prep Time: 25 minutes | Cook Time: 13 minutes

Nothing beats a savory filled tortilla with lean protein in the morning. If you love vitamin packed veggies, ooey gooey cheese, and a little spice to jump start your day—these Breakfast Burritos are just perfect! These healthy burritos seem sinful but are packed full of a super-food boost to help curb cravings until lunch.

Ingredients:

1 tablespoon olive oil

1/4 cup red onion, diced

1 cup red pepper, seeded and diced

1 (15-ounce) can black beans, drained and rinsed

1/4 teaspoon red pepper flakes

1/8 teaspoon sea salt

1/8 teaspoon fresh ground black pepper

4 large eggs and 4 egg whites

1 cup pepper jack cheese, shredded

Cooking spray

4 flour tortillas (burrito-size), made using Victoria Cast Iron tortilla press

1 avocado, diced

Sour cream, for garnish

Pico de gallo, for garnish

Hot sauce, for garnish

Flour Tortillas:

1 cup all-purpose flour

3 teaspoons vegetable shortening, chilled

1/4 teaspoon sea salt

1/2 teaspoon baking powder

1/2 cup water

Sheet of plastic ziploc bag (cut in half)

[please see page 31 for instructions]

Instructions:

1. Heat the olive oil in a large nonstick frying pan over a medium-high heat. Cook the onions and peppers 5-7 minutes until onions are softened.

2. Add black beans and red pepper to frying pan. Cook for an additional 3 minutes. Season with salt and pepper and transfer to a bowl.

3. Whisk together the eggs and egg whites in a large mixing bowl. Fold in the cheese.

4. Spray the frying pan with cooking spray, and reheat the pan over a medium heat. Reduce heat to low. Add eggs and scramble for 3 minutes until cooked through.

5. Spread 1 tablespoon each of sour cream and salsa down the middle of each tortilla. Layer with 1/4 of the black bean mix, 1/4 scrambled eggs, pico de gallo, avocado and garnish with hot sauce.

6. Fold into a burrito and serve!

Nutritional Info: Calories: 427 | Sodium: 295 mg | Dietary Fiber 10.9 g | Total Fat: 19.5 g | Total Carbs: 42.0 g | Protein: 23.1 g.

Chicken and Avocado Burritos

Servings: 6 | Prep Time: 10 minutes | Cook Time: 20 minutes

Cool creamy burritos are just the thing to hit the spot when it comes to stuffing fresh, flour tortillas. You can even grill these burritos for about three minutes on each side for a flavor packed, toasted treat! Serve these burritos up with chips and salsa for one tasty healthy meal.

Ingredients:

6 flour tortillas, warmed

1 pound cooked chicken, sliced or shredded

1 large avocado, diced

1 cup monterey jack cheese, shredded

1/4 cup salsa verde

1/4 cup sour cream or greek yogurt

2 tablespoons cilantro, chopped

6 flour tortillas, made using Victoria Cast Iron tortilla press

Flour Tortillas:

2 cups all-purpose flour

4 1/2 teaspoons vegetable shortening, chilled

1/2 teaspoon sea salt

1 teaspoon baking powder

2/3 cups water

Sheet of plastic ziploc bag (cut in half)

[please see page 31 for instructions]

Instructions:

1.   Lay tortillas on a flat work surface.

2. Spread a thin layer of sour cream over half of each tortilla. Add a 1/2 tablespoon of cilantro on each layer of sour cream. Top with 1/2 cup cheese. Spread an even layer of chicken, avocado and salsa down the middle of each burrito.

3. Wrap the sour cream side up and over the meaty stuffing. Fold each end in and continue rolling until fully wrapped. Enjoy!

Nutritional Info: Calories: 457, Sodium: 372 mg, Dietary Fiber: 3.4 g, Total Fat: 20.2 g, Total Carbs: 36.1 g, Protein: 31.9 g.

Chorizo Migas

Servings: 6-8 | Prep Time: 10 minutes | Cook Time: 20 minutes

Whip up Chorizo Migas and put a modern twist on this ancient dish from Spain and Portugal. Chorizo Migas make for one fresh dish for breakfast, brunch, or even dinner! Top with fresh salsa for one seriously sweet kick.

Ingredients:

8 ounces chorizo, casings removed and crumbled

1 large onion, chopped

2 poblano peppers, chopped

5 corn tortillas, torn into bite-size pieces, made using Victoria Cast Iron tortilla press

1 (32-ounce) carton liquid egg substitute, such as Egg Beaters

1/2 teaspoon dried oregano

1/2 teaspoon salt

1/2 teaspoon freshly ground pepper

1/2 cup chopped cilantro, plus more for garnish

Salsa, for garnish

Corn Tortillas:

1/2 cup masa harina

1/2 teaspoon sea salt

1/2 cup hot water

Sheet of plastic ziploc bag (cut in half)

[please see page 29 for instructions]

Ingredients:

1. Heat a frying pan on medium. Cook chorizo, onion and peppers for 6-9 minutes stirring occasionally, until the chorizo is cooked and the vegetables are softened. Transfer to a paper towel lined plate.

2.   Discard all but 1 tablespoon of fat from the pan. Add the tortilla pieces and cook 4-6 minutes, over medium heat, stirring often, until they begin to brown.

3.   Whisk egg substitute, oregano, salt and pepper in a medium bowl. Add the egg mixture and the reserved chorizo mixture to the frying pan; cook 4-6 minutes, stirring occasionally, until the eggs are set. Remove from the heat and fold in cilantro.

4.   Serve with a side of salsa and more cilantro.

Nutritional Info: Calories: 241 | Sodium: 725 mg | Dietary Fiber 1.8 g | Total Fat: 11.4 g | Total Carbs: 12.3 g | Protein: 22.0 g.

Coconut Blueberry Parcels

Servings: 3 | Prep Time: 10 minutes | Cook Time: 14 minutes

Whip up one sincerely amazing protein loaded, gluten-free breakfast or brunch treat with these scrumptious Coconut Blueberry Parcels. Loaded with antioxidant rich blueberries, these sweet parcels are also paleo and clean eating friendly! Serve them up with side of fresh fruit and spa water and treat yourself as you start the day.

Ingredients:

2 tablespoon coconut flour

2 tablespoon oat flour

2 tablespoons vanilla whey protein powder

2 tablespoons shredded coconut

1 teaspoon sugar substitute

4 tablespoons almond milk, unsweetened

1/2 cup fresh blueberries

2 tablespoons water

3 corn tortillas, made using Victoria Cast Iron tortilla press

Corn Tortillas:

1/2 cup masa harina

1/2 teaspoon sea salt

1/2 cup hot water

Sheet of plastic ziploc bag (cut in half)

[please see page 29 for instructions]

Instructions:

1. Combine coconut flour, oat flour, vanilla whey, shredded coconut and sugar substitute in a mixing bowl.

2. Whisk in almond milk until a paste forms and set aside.

3. Add half the blueberries to separate mixing bowl with water. Microwave for 30 seconds.

4. Lay the tortillas on a flat surface. Distribute half the filling into the middle of both. Top each with microwaved blueberries. Add the remainder of the filling. Top with remainder of fresh blueberries. Fold the sides to make a square shape parcel; repeat with second tortilla.

5. Heat a frying pan on medium. Spray with cooking spray and lay both tortilla parcels seam side down.

6. Cook until crispy on the base, about 5-7 minutes. Flip and cook for another 5-7 minutes until golden crisp; repeat on the other side. Serve immediately and enjoy.

Nutritional Info: Calories: 275 | Sodium: 54 mg | Dietary Fiber 4.3 g | Total Fat: 11.1 g | Total Carbs: 31.3 g | Protein: 15.0 g.

Curried Tuna Wraps

Servings: 2 | Prep Time: 10 minutes

Spice things up with warm curry and whip up something fresh with your freshly made tortillas. Tuna is so delicious and nutritious, and what better way to enjoy lunch on the go than with these scrumptious Curried Tuna Wraps! Enjoy with fresh fruit on the side for one super-clean meal.

Ingredients:

1 (5-ounce) can tuna in water, drained

1/4 cup sunflower seeds

2 tablespoons garlic, minced

1 teaspoon lemon juice

2 tablespoons dried currants

3 tablespoons chickpeas, rinsed and drained and coarsely chopped

2 teaspoons mild curry powder

1/4 cup sugar-free mayonnaise

1/4 teaspoon sea salt

4 leaves romaine lettuce

4 corn tortillas, made using Victoria Cast Iron tortilla press

Corn Tortillas:

1 cup masa harina

1 teaspoon sea salt

1 cup hot water

Sheet of plastic ziploc bag (cut in half)

[please see page 29 for instructions]

Instructions:

1. Combine tuna, sunflower seeds, garlic, currants, chickpeas, lemon juice, curry powder, mayonnaise, salt in a large mixing bowl.

2. Lay tortillas out flat. Place one leaf of lettuce in center of each tortilla.

3.   Spread 1/4 cup of tuna mixture into the leaf.

4.   Fold in one side of the tortilla edges around the leaf, enclosing the tuna within it like a burrito. Cut each wrap in half crosswise, on a diagonal, and serve with fresh fruit or carrot sticks.

Nutritional Info: Calories: 437 | Sodium: 509 mg | Dietary Fiber: 8.0 g | Total Fat: 17.7 g | Total Carbs: 46.2 g | Protein: 25.5 g.

Eight Layer Chicken Chili Dip

Servings: 10 | Prep Time: 15 minutes | Cook Time: 30 minutes, plus 2 - 24 hours

Spice up any party or family fun night with Eight Layer Chicken Dip. Get the whole family in the kitchen and prep it together. Then serve with fresh tortilla chips made with the help of your Victoria Cast Iron Tortilla Press.

Ingredients:

1/2 cup and 1 tablespoon olive oil

10 corn tortillas, cut into triangles; made using Victoria Cast Iron tortilla press

1 medium onion, chopped

2 cloves garlic, finely chopped

3 tablespoons ancho chili paste

1 tablespoon chili powder

1/4 teaspoon sea salt

1/4 teaspoon cayenne pepper

1 cup low-sodium chicken broth

2 cups chicken, shredded

1 cup sour cream

1 cup cilantro, chopped

1 lime, juice and zested

1 (16-ounce) can black beans, drained and rinsed

1 can green chilies, chopped

1 1/2 cups cornbread, crumbled

2 medium tomatoes, diced

1 1/2 cups cheddar cheese, shredded

Corn Tortillas:

1 cup masa harina

1 teaspoon sea salt

1 cup hot water

Sheet of plastic ziploc bag (cut in half)

[please see page 29 for instructions]

Instructions:

1. Heat 1/2 cup olive oil in a large frying pan on medium-high heat. Fry corn tortillas triangles in a single layer for three to five minutes on each side, until golden and crisp.

2. Transfer to a paper towel lined plate to degrease and cool.

3. Drain oil and return frying pan to medium-high heat. Add 1 tablespoon olive oil. Add the garlic and half of the onion. Cook for 4 minutes, until softened and starting to brown.

4. Add the chili paste, chili powder, sea salt and cayenne pepper. Cook for three minutes; stirring constantly until the oil is deep brown.

5. Fold in the chicken broth and bring to a simmer. Cook for three minutes until thickened.

6. Stir in the shredded chicken and cook for five minutes. Remove from heat and cool to room temperature.

7. Whisk sour cream, cilantro, lime juice and zest in a small mixing bowl.

8. Add green chilies and pepper to another small mixing bowl and toss well.

9. Layer the dip in a medium glass trifle bowl or a deep serving dish. Spread the cornbread on the bottom, top with an even layer of chopped tomatoes, then beans, next cheese, a layer of cilantro lime sour cream, chicken chili, the remaining chopped onions and the chili pepper mix.

10. Cover with plastic wrap and refrigerate until well chilled for 2 to 24 hours; the longer it is refrigerated, the more delicious it will be as all the flavors will set nicely.

11. Serve with fresh tortilla chips for dipping!

Nutritional Info: Calories: 576 | Sodium: 507 mg | Dietary Fiber: 10.9 g | Total Fat: 27.1 g | Total Carbs: 58.8 g | Protein: 27.7 g.

Endive Quesadillas

Servings: 4-6 | Prep Time: 20 minutes | Cook Time: 35 minutes

Spice things up with veggies and wilted endive stuffed quesadillas. The spicy chicory flavored endive packs a mean punch when it comes to vegetarian food with flare.

Ingredients:

1 pound endive

6 tablespoons extra-virgin olive oil

3 cloves garlic, minced

3/4 teaspoons sea salt

1/4 teaspoon ground black pepper

1 tablespoon hot sauce, like Tabasco

8 flour tortillas, made using Victoria Cast Iron tortilla press

4 cups mozzarella cheese, shredded

1 (15-ounce) can black beans, rinsed and drained

1 medium tomato, diced

1 tablespoon fresh lime juice

3/4 teaspoons ground cumin

Salsa, for serving

Flour Tortillas:

2 cups all-purpose flour

4 1/2 teaspoons vegetable shortening, chilled

1/2 teaspoon sea salt

1 teaspoon baking powder

2/3 cups water

Sheet of plastic ziploc bag (cut in half)

[please see page 31 for instructions]

Instructions:

1.   Wash the endive and tear into bite-size pieces.

2. Heat 1 tablespoon of the olive oil in a large nonstick frying pan over medium heat until hot. Stir in the garlic, 3/4 teaspoons salt and 1/4 teaspoon pepper. Cook for 2 minutes, stirring, until the garlic is toasted.

3. Stir in the torn endive. Cook 5 minutes, turning with tongs and adding more endive as the greens wilt; until the liquid evaporates. Then stir in the hot sauce, cumin, black beans and tomato.

4. Place 4 tortillas on a flat work surface. Spread a 1/2 cup of the cheese evenly over each tortilla, then divide the endive mix among the tortillas, spreading evenly. Sprinkle the endive mix with 1/2 cup more cheese per tortilla. Top with the remaining tortillas.

5. Wipe out the frying pan with a paper towel. Heat remaining tablespoon of oil over medium heat.

6. Place 1 quesadilla in the skillet and cover. Cook until the bottom is golden, 2 to 3 minutes. Flip the tortilla and cook until the other side is golden, 2 to 3 minutes more.

7. Transfer the quesadilla to a work surface and tent with aluminum foil. Repeat until all quesadillas are cooked.

8. Cut the quesadillas into wedges and serve salsa.

Nutritional Info: Calories: 665 | Sodium: 553 mg | Dietary Fiber 15.5 g | Total Fat: 29.5 g | Total Carbs: 65.3 g | Protein: 39.8 g.

Fresh Tuna Tortillas

Servings: 4 | Prep Time: 10 minutes | Cook Time: 10 minutes

Add some omega-3 rich protein to your clean eating diet with these delicious Fresh Tuna Tortillas. You'll love the super fresh taste of tuna stuffed into fresh pressed tortillas using your Victoria Cast Iron Tortilla Press. Serve them up with a garden salad for one killer healthy meal.

Ingredients:

1 tablespoon olive oil

2 large tuna steaks

1 pinch cayenne pepper

1/8 teaspoon sea salt

1 teaspoon ground cumin

4 corn tortillas, made using Victoria Cast Iron tortilla press

1 avocado, sliced

2 tomatoes, diced

1 lime, cut into wedges

2 tablespoons cilantro, chopped

Soured cream, for garnish

Corn Tortillas:

1/2 cup masa harina

1/2 teaspoon sea salt

1/2 cup hot water

Sheet of plastic ziploc bag (cut in half)

[please see page 29 for instructions]

Instructions:

1. Combine tuna steaks, olive oil and spices in a mixing bowl; toss well to coat. Heat a griddle or grill pan until on medium heat until hot. Sear the steaks on one side for 2 mins. Flip and sear for 1-2 minutes more.

2. Transfer tuna steaks to a cutting board and cut crosswise into 1-inch strips.

3. Heat the tortillas for 30 secs in a microwave until soft.

4. Pile tuna, avocado and tomatoes on top of each tortilla. Squeeze a lime wedge over the tuna mix. Top with cilantro and a dollop of sour cream. Roll up like a burrito and enjoy!

Nutritional Info: Calories: 276 | Sodium: 194 mg | Dietary Fiber 5.8 g | Total Fat: 16.9 g | Total Carbs: 18.3 g | Protein: 15.5 g.

Fruit-Filled French Toast Wraps

Servings: 4 | Prep Time: 10 minutes | Cook Time: 10 minutes

For those days, you want to indulge, stuff some french toast wraps full of fruit for one sweet treat! Sure, to become a favorite staple for brunch, this delicious recipe is fabulous served with a side of turkey bacon, sausage, and a mimosa.

Ingredients:

2 large eggs

1/4 cup ultra-filtered 2% milk, like Fair Life

1 teaspoon ground cinnamon

1/2 teaspoon ground nutmeg

3/4 cups greek vanilla yogurt

2/3 cups sliced ripe banana

4 corn tortillas, made using Victoria Cast Iron tortilla press

2 teaspoons butter

2/3 cups sliced fresh strawberries

2/3 cups fresh blueberries

Powdered sugar, for dusting

Corn Tortillas:

1/2 cup masa harina

1/2 teaspoon sea salt

1/2 cup hot water

Sheet of plastic ziploc bag (cut in half)

[please see page 29 for instructions]

Instructions:

1. Whisk egg, milk, cinnamon and nutmeg together in a shallow mixing bowl. Set aside to rest.

2. Mash a ripe banana in a separate mixing bowl and fold in yogurt until smooth.

3. Heat butter over medium-high heat on a griddle or flat frying pan.

91

4.   Submerge one tortilla in the egg wash. Shake off excess and transfer to griddle for 2 minutes, flip and fry an additional 2 minutes until golden brown. Repeat for second tortilla.

5.   Lay tortilla flat on a plate. Spoon yogurt mixture down middle of each tortilla.

6.   Top yogurt with 1/3 strawberries and blueberries.

7.   Roll them up like a burrito. Dust with powdered sugar and serve!

Nutritional Info: Calories: 331 | Sodium: 188 mg | Dietary Fiber: 5.7 g | Total Fat: 11.9 g | Total Carbs: 42.4 g | Protein: 15.3 g.

Salmon and Egg Wraps

Servings: 4 | Prep Time: 20 minutes | Cook Time: 15 minutes

Lean protein load with these delicious Salmon and Egg Wraps. Create a "load your own" style brunch by setting all the ingredients out buffet style for friends to assemble their own. These wraps are also great to make ahead, slice into 2 inch rings, secure with a toothpick—and you've got salmon and egg party bites!

Ingredients:

1 large egg

8 slices smoked salmon

1 cup baby spinach

4 flour tortillas, made using Victoria Cast Iron tortilla press

For the Mustard Mayo:

1/2 cup sugar-free mayonnaise, like Duke's

3 teaspoons Dijon mustard

1 tablespoon Worcestershire sauce

1/2 teaspoon sugar substitute, like Splenda

1/2 teaspoon garlic, minced

Flour Tortillas:

1 cup all-purpose flour

3 teaspoons vegetable shortening, chilled

1/4 teaspoon sea salt

1/2 teaspoon baking powder

1/2 cup water

sheet of plastic ziploc bag (cut in half)

[please see page 31 for instructions]

Instructions:

1. Combine all of the ingredients for the mustard mayo in a mixing bowl. Cover with plastic wrap and set in the refrigerator to chill.

2. Bring 2 quarts of water to a hard boil in a large sauce pot. Carefully add the 6 eggs. Boil for 10 minutes.

3. Remove eggs from hot water and immediately place in an ice bath for 3 to 5 minutes.

4. Crack eggs. Remove shell and rinse. Slice into thin slices. Place slices on a plate. Cover with plastic wrap and set in the refrigerator to chill while you assemble your wrap.

5. Spread a layer of the mustard mayo onto each wrap. Add 2 slices of smoked salmon, two to three slices of hard-boiled egg, and a helping of spinach to each. Roll up tightly.

6. Cut each wrap on the diagonal into two pieces. Serve with the extra mustard mayo on the side for dipping.

Nutritional Info: Calories: 107 | Sodium: 634 mg | Dietary Fiber 1.7 g | Total Fat: 3.2 g | Total Carbs: 11.1 g | Protein: 8.6 g.

Salsa Chicken & Cheese Tortillas

Servings: 3 | Prep Time: 10 minutes | Cook Time: 6 minutes

Want to whip up something quick and filling for a packed lunch? These Salsa Chicken and Cheese Tortillas will totally hit the spot. Take them to work or send them to school alongside carrot sticks and yogurt.

Ingredients:

4 tablespoons hot salsa

3 flour tortillas, made using Victoria Cast Iron tortilla press

1 (15-ounce) can kidney beans, drained, rinsed and roughly mashed

1 spring onion, chopped

1 cup leftover roast chicken, shredded

1 cup cheddar cheese, shredded

2 tablespoons cilantro, chopped

Olive oil, for brushing

Flour Tortillas:

1 cup all-purpose flour

3 teaspoons vegetable shortening, chilled

1/4 teaspoon sea salt

1/2 teaspoon baking powder

1/2 cup water

Sheet of plastic ziploc bag (cut in half)

[please see page 31 for instructions]

Instructions:

1. Brush each tortilla on one side with olive oil. Lay it oil side down on parchment paper to fill.

2.	Spread 2 tablespoons salsa onto each tortilla. Top each with an even layer of the beans, spring onion, chicken and cheddar. Sprinkle cilantro on both. Fold each tortilla in half and gently press to flatten.

3.	Heat a large non-stick frying pan on medium. Cook the tortilla on both sides for 4 minutes each, until cheese is melted.

4.	Cut into wedges and serve.

Nutritional Info: Calories: 1141 | Sodium: 641 mg | Dietary Fiber 34.6 g | Total Fat: 26.9 g |
Total Carbs: 144.3 g | Protein: 84.2 g.

Smothered Green Chile Breakfast Burritos

Servings: 4 | Prep Time: 10 minutes | Cook Time: 60 minutes

Smothered and cover your breakfast burrito with spicy, but mild, green chili sauce. These mouthwatering breakfast burritos are just the thing to help you kick start your day the healthy way!

Ingredients:

For Green Chile Sauce:

2 teaspoons olive oil

3/4 cups onion, minced

2 cloves garlic, minced

1 tablespoon all-purpose flour

3 (4-ounce) cans green chilies

2 cups reduced-sodium chicken broth

For Burritos:

3 slices bacon

1/2 cup onion, chopped

1 clove garlic, minced

4 cups frozen hash browns

2 large eggs, lightly beaten

4 flour tortillas, made using Victoria Cast Iron tortilla press

3/4 cups Cheddar cheese, shredded

Flour Tortillas:

1 cup all-purpose flour

3 teaspoons vegetable shortening, chilled

1/4 teaspoon sea salt

1/2 teaspoon baking powder

1/2 cup water

Sheet of plastic ziploc bag (cut in half)

[please see page 31 for   instructions]

Instructions:

1.   For chili sauce: Heat oil in a medium saucepan over medium heat. Add minced onion and garlic. Cook 4 minutes, stirring, until very soft. Sprinkle flour over the mixture and cook, stirring, for 1 minute more. Add chilies and broth; bring to a boil. Reduce heat to a low simmer and cook until thickened; 15-20 minutes. Set aside.

2.   For the Burritos: Cook bacon in a large frying pan over medium-high heat until crisp, about 4 minutes. Transfer to a paper towel lined plate. Chop when cooled.

3.   Add chopped onion and garlic to the pan and cook, stirring, for 1 minute. Stir in potatoes. Pat the mixture down evenly with a spatula and cook, without stirring, for 2 minutes. Scrape up the browned bits, flip and pat back down again; continue cooking without stirring for about 2 minutes more. Repeat again, for 2 more minutes, until the potatoes are golden brown with some crisp edges.

4.   Put green chili sauce back on the stove on low heat.

5.   Reduce heat to low. Stir 1/4 cup sauce and eggs into the potato mixture and cook, stirring frequently, until the eggs are just set, 1 to 2 minutes. Stir in the bacon and warm through for 1 minute.

6.   Divide the mixture evenly among tortillas. Roll each into a burrito and arrange seam-down on plates. Spoon warm chili sauce over the burritos, sprinkle with cheese and serve.

Nutritional Info: Calories: 521 | Sodium: 1165 mg | Dietary Fiber 5.4 g | Total Fat: 26.0 g | Total Carbs: 55.5 g | Protein: 15.6 g.

Spinach and Feta Quesadillas

Servings: 4 | Prep Time: 10 minutes | Cook Time: 25 minutes

Go totally Greek with your Victoria Cast Iron Tortilla Press and whip up some fresh quesadillas. Healthy, nutritious, and packed full of super-food vitamins and minerals— Spinach and Feta Quesadillas are beautiful served with an heirloom tomato salad or roasted sweet potatoes on the side.

Ingredients:

1 tablespoon olive oil

1/4 cup red onion, finely chopped

2 cups spinach, chopped

2/3 cups feta, crumbled

1/4 cup black olives, sliced

4 corn tortillas, made using Victoria Cast Iron tortilla press

Greek dressing, for dipping

Corn Tortillas:

1/2 cup masa harina

1/2 teaspoon sea salt

1/2 cup hot water

Sheet of plastic ziploc bag (cut in half)

[please see page 29 for instructions]

Ingredients:

1. Warm olive oil in a frying pan on medium-high heat. Add onion and cook 3 minutes; until softened.

2. Stir in spinach and cook for 3 minutes stirring constantly. Transfer to a mixing bowl.

3. Fold cheese and olives into the mixing bowl.

4. Spread spinach mix over one half of each tortilla. Fold in half and press lightly to seal.

5.   Heat a large frying pan or griddle over medium-high heat. Cook quesadillas for 6 to 8 minutes each, one at a time, turning once, until golden brown on both sides and cheese is melted. Serve with your favorite side and a small bowl of greek dressing for dipping.

Nutritional Info: Calories: 164 | Sodium: 375 mg | Dietary Fiber: 2.3 g | Total Fat: 10.5 g | Total Carbs: 13.5 g | Protein: 5.5 g.

Spinach Tomato Quesadilla with Pesto

Servings: 2 | Prep Time: 10 minutes | Cook Time: 20 minutes

Looking for a fun, easy recipe to start out your tortilla making adventure—then you'll love these delicious, healthy Spinach Tomato Quesadillas with Pesto! Turn them into a Vegan meal option by using dairy-free cheese and pesto or a gluten-free meal using corn tortillas.

Ingredients:

1 roma tomato, thinly sliced

1/2 cup baby spinach

1 jar of traditional pesto sauce

1 cup feta cheese crumbles

1 cup mozzarella cheese, shredded

2 large flour tortilla, made using Victoria Cast Iron tortilla press

Flour Tortillas:

1 cup all-purpose flour

3 teaspoons vegetable shortening, chilled

1/4 teaspoon sea salt

1/2 teaspoon baking powder

1/2 cup water

Sheet of plastic ziploc bag (cut in half)

[please see page 31 for instructions]

Directions:

1. Pre-heat a large frying pan on medium heat.
2. Spread a thin layer of pesto on one side of each tortilla.
3. Add 1/4 cup of mozzarella and feta to two tortillas.
4. Top with an even layer of tomato slices and spinach. Top spinach with the rest of the feta and mozzarella. Place a tortilla on top of the cheese layer, pesto side down.

5.   Spray frying pan with a thin layer of cooking spray. Cook each quesadilla for 5 minutes, flip, and heat for another 5 minutes; until cheese has melted.

6.   Cut into triangles and serve hot!

Nutritional Info: Calories: 1115, Sodium: 1747 mg, Dietary Fiber: 5.7 g, Total Fat: 79.4 g, Total Carbs: 61.5 g, Protein: 44.5 g.

Tortilla French Toast

Servings: 4 | Prep Time: 10 minutes | Cook Time: 5 minutes

Whip up some Tortilla French Toast for one simple way to indulge a little. Delicious, nutritious and healthy, our twist on this infamous breakfast item has never been so easy! Enjoy it as an afternoon snack or dessert too—for those who live to indulge their sweet tooth.

Ingredients:

2 large eggs

1/2 cup 2% ultra-filtered milk, like Fair Life

1 tablespoon pure vanilla extract

1/4 cup sugar substitute, like Splenda

2 teaspoons ground cinnamon

1 tablespoon butter, unsalted

4 corn tortillas, made using Victoria Cast Iron tortilla press

Maple syrup, optional topping

Powdered sugar, optional topping

Strawberries, optional topping

Corn Tortillas:

1/2 cup masa harina

1/2 teaspoon sea salt

1/2 cup hot water

Sheet of plastic ziploc bag (cut in half)

[please see page 29 for instructions]

Instructions:

1. Whisk the egg, milk and vanilla together in a large mixing bowl.
2. Blend the sugar substitute and cinnamon together in a large, shallow mixing bowl.

3. Heat a cast iron skillet or griddle on medium heat. Add the butter to melt or brush it onto the griddle.

4. Fold a tortilla in half, then in half again and submerge it into the egg mixture until well-coated.

5. Unfold the tortilla and shake off the excess egg mix.

6. Dredge the tortilla in the cinnamon sugar mix. Coat both sides well.

7. Repeat the coating process for all tortillas.

8. Place each tortilla onto the pan or hot griddle. Fry the tortillas for 2 minutes on each side, until they puff up and begin to turn golden-brown.

9. Fold in half again, and in half again to make a triangle. Top with maple syrup, powdered sugar or your favorite fruit.

Nutritional Info: Calories: 201 | Sodium: 81 mg | Dietary Fiber: 2.1 g | Total Fat: 6.7 g | Total Carbs: 25.7 g | Protein: 5.6 g.

Waffled Chorizo & Cheese Quesadilla

Servings: 2-4 | Prep Time: 15 minutes | Cook Time: 15 minutes

What could be better than a delicious waffled quesadilla stuffed with copious amounts of melted cheese and warm, spicy chorizo!? Nothing. When you are craving comfort food, this delicious recipe hits the spot. Serve it up for brunch with a side of scrambled eggs, fresh fruit and french toast tortillas for one amazing mid-day of tortilla filled fun.

Ingredients:

1 lime, juiced

1/4 small red onion, thinly sliced

Pinch sea salt

3 tablespoons olive oil

2 ounces' fresh chorizo, chopped

4 flour tortillas, made using Victoria Cast Iron tortilla press

2/3 cups cheddar, shredded

Fresh salsa, for garnish

Sour cream, for garnish

Chopped avocado, for garnish

Flour Tortillas:

3 1/2 cups all-purpose flour

3 tablespoons vegetable shortening, chilled

1 teaspoon sea salt

2 teaspoons baking powder

1 1/2 cup water

[please see page 31 for instructions]

Instructions

1. Combine the lime juice, onions and salt in a small metal mixing bowl. Let sit for 20 minutes, at room temperature, until the onions are pink.

2. Heat a frying pan over medium-high heat. Add the chorizo and cook until browned, about 3 minutes. Transfer to a paper towel lined plate cool.

3. Preheat a waffle iron to medium-high. Brush one side of all the tortillas with oil and lay dry-side up on a flat surface.

4. Sprinkle 1/3 cup cheese on the tortilla in the waffle iron, then a scoop of pickled onions and a sprinkle of chorizo. Place a second tortilla on top olive oil brushed side up.

5. Close the waffle iron gently and cook for 4 to 6 minutes until golden brown and the cheese is melted; repeat with the remaining quesadilla.

6. Cut the quesadillas into triangles. Serve with salsa, sour cream and avocado on the side.

Nutritional Info: Calories: 246 | Sodium: 360 mg | Dietary Fiber: 2.1 g | Total Fat: 18.0 g | Total Carbs: 13.6 g | Protein: 9.5 g.

Wrap Sandwich

Toss traditional bread aside with your Victoria Cast Iron Tortilla Press and wrap your sandwiches in fresh pressed tortillas. Perfect for a grab and go style lunch or take away lunch, the Wrap Sandwich will surely become your favorite, healthy way to curb hunger during the day!

Ingredients:

4 corn or flour tortillas., made using Victoria Cast Iron tortilla press

8 leaves romaine lettuce, rinsed and trimmed

1/2-pound turkey breast, sliced

12 slices apple-wood smoked bacon, cooked

1 vine-ripened tomato, diced

1 ripe avocado, peeled, pitted and cut into thin slices

2 teaspoons lime juice

1/8 teaspoon sea salt

1/8 teaspoon fresh ground pepper

1/2 cup sugar-free mayonnaise

Corn Tortillas:

1/2 cup masa harina

1/2 teaspoon sea salt

1/2 cup hot water

Sheet of plastic ziploc bag (cut in half)

[please see page 29 for instructions]

Instructions:

1. Wrap the tortillas in barely damp, paper towels and microwave on high for 30 seconds.

2.   Lay the tortillas on a flat work surface. Lay two pieces of lettuce in the middle of each tortilla. Top lettuce with a few turkey slices. Follow with two slices of bacon, some diced tomato and avocado slices. Season with salt and pepper. Top with a squeeze of mayonnaise.

3.   Fold up the bottom quarter of the tortilla and roll each sandwich into a cone shape. Secure the tortilla with a toothpick. Serve immediately.

Nutritional Info: Calories: 437 | Sodium: 1239 mg | Dietary Fiber 5.5 g | Total Fat: 29.2 g | Total Carbs: 26.2 g | Protein: 19.5 g.

9

Classic Tortilla Snacks

Baked Tortilla Chips

Servings: 5 | Prep Time: 7 minutes | Cook Time: 20 minutes

Turn your culinary skills up a notch and learn how to bake your very own healthy, delicious tortilla chips! Serve them up for parties or movie night. Don't forget the salsa, hummus, queso—or whatever kind of dip your tortilla chip loving heart desires!

Ingredients:

16 corn tortillas, made using Victoria Cast Iron tortilla press

3 tablespoons olive oil

1 tablespoon cumin

1 tablespoon chili powder, mild

1 tablespoon smoked paprika

1 teaspoon kosher salt

1/2 teaspoon black pepper

Corn Tortillas:

2 cups masa harina

1/2 tablespoon sea salt

1 1/2 cups hot water

sheet of plastic ziploc bag (cut in half)

[please see page 29 for instructions]

Instructions:

1. Pre-heat oven to 350 degrees Fahrenheit.
2. Line two baking sheets with aluminum foil.
3. Use a pizza cutter to cut the tortillas into 4 triangles, then cut each large triangle in half to create 8 triangles per tortilla.
4. Toss the triangles in olive oil; coat well. Toss the oiled triangles in spices and mix well with your hands.
5. Spread the tortilla triangles evenly across the baking sheets in one even layer.

6.   Bake for 18-25 minutes or until golden brown.

7.   Serve with your favorite dip. Store leftovers in an airtight container for up to four days.

Nutritional Info: Calories: 264 | Sodium: 636 mg | Dietary Fiber: 6.1 g | Total Fat: 13.4 g | Total Carbs: 35.0 g | Protein: 4.9 g.

Bean and Cheese Taquitos

Servings: 4 | Prep Time: 25 minutes | Cook Time: 25 minutes

Snack healthy with scrumptious Bean & Cheese Taquitos. Great for those who love to clean eat or are Vegetarian conscious, these taquitos combine savory beans with gooey cheese for one scrumptious snack! Serve them alongside sangria or lemonade on the patio for some fun snacking in the sun.

Ingredients:

1 cup black beans, rinsed

1/2 cup monterey jack cheese, shredded

1 teaspoon sea salt

8 corn tortillas, made using Victoria Cast Iron tortilla press

3/4 cups olive oil

1/2 cup salsa

1/4 cup sour cream

1/2 cup guacamole

Corn Tortillas:

1 cup masa harina

1 teaspoon sea salt

1 cup hot water

Sheet of plastic ziploc bag (cut in half)

[please see page 29 for instructions]

Instructions:

1. Add the black beans, monterey jack and sea salt to a mixing bowl. Mash the mix gently for two minutes.

2. Lay tortillas flat and divide the bean and cheese mix evenly into the middle of each tortilla. Roll each tortilla up tight and skinny.

3.   Heat the olive oil in a large frying pan over medium high heat. Place four to rolls into the hot oil, seam side down, and fry 2 to 3 minutes per side until golden crisp.

4.   Transfer to a paper towel lined plate to cool. Cook remaining taquitos. Serve with the salsa, sour cream and guacamole.

Nutritional Info: Calories: 728 | Sodium: 857 mg | Dietary Fiber: 11.9 g | Total Fat: 51.2 g | Total Carbs: 56.4 g | Protein: 18.1 g.

Cheese and Chile Melts

Servings: 8 | Prep Time: 15 minutes | Cook Time: 6 minutes

Whip up some quick and easy cheesy filled melts with savory green chilies tonight. When it comes to getting creative with your fresh pressed Victoria Cast Iron Tortillas, this is a great way to get started. A quick and easy snack, these Cheese and Chile Melts can also be turned into a healthy meal with a side of fresh fruit and yogurt.

Ingredients:

2 cups cheddar, grated

4 tomatoes, chopped

1 (4-ounce) can green chilies

1/4 cup cilantro, chopped

8 flour tortillas, made using Victoria Cast Iron tortilla press

Olive oil, for brushing

Flour Tortillas:

2 cups all-purpose flour

4 1/2 teaspoons vegetable shortening, chilled

1/2 teaspoon sea salt

1 teaspoon baking powder

2/3 cups water

Sheet of plastic ziploc bag (cut in half)

[please see page 31 for instructions]

Instructions:

1. Combine the cheese, tomatoes, chili and cilantro in a mixing bowl.

2. Warm tortillas individually, for 5 seconds each, in a microwave.

3. Lay warmed tortillas on a flat work surface. Divide the cheese mix over one half of each tortilla. Fold tortillas in half to make 8 half-moons, then press gently to flatten.

4. Heat a frying pan or grill on medium high heat.

5. Brush the tops with olive oil, then sit and place oil side down in heated surface. Cook for 3 minutes. Brush the uncooked side with oil, then flip over for another 3mins. Cook until golden crisp and cheese is melted.

6. Slice into wedges and serve!

Nutritional Info: Calories: 117 | Sodium: 244 mg | Dietary Fiber 2.3 g | Total Fat: 2.8 g | Total Carbs: 14.6 g | Protein: 8.8 g.

Cheesy Corn and Black Bean Quesadillas

Servings: 6-8 | Prep Time: 15 minutes | Cook Time: 20 minutes

When it comes to quesadillas this recipe is super simple and stuffed with all the ooey gooey cheese your quesadilla loving heart desires. Perfect for those who love to eat vegetarian or just love clean eating with fresh made tortillas. These quesadillas can also be kept in the refrigerator for a few days, and warmed up for lunch the next day in a toaster oven or microwave.

Ingredients:

- 1 tablespoon olive oil
- 1 small onion, chopped
- 1 jalapeño, seeded and finely chopped
- 2 cloves garlic, minced
- 1 (15 1/2-ounce) can black beans, rinsed and drained
- 1 1/2 cups frozen corn kernels, thawed
- 3/4 cups pepper jack cheese, shredded
- 1 teaspoon sea salt
- 1 teaspoon coarse black pepper
- 8 corn tortillas, made using Victoria Cast Iron tortilla press
- Salsa, for garnish
- Sour cream, for garnish

Corn Tortillas:

- 1 cup masa harina
- 1 teaspoon sea salt
- 1 cup hot water
- Sheet of plastic ziploc bag (cut in half)
- [please see page 29 for instructions]

Instructions:

1. Preheat an oven to 200ºF.

2. Mash black beans with a potato masher in a large mixing bowl.

3. Heat a large frying pan over medium-high heat. Add corn kernels and cook for 3 to 4 minutes, stirring occasionally, until corn begins to brown. Transfer corn to mixing bowl with beans.

4. Add oil to the frying pan, and heat for 3 minutes. Add onion and jalapeño. Sauté for 5 minutes. Add garlic and sauté 2 minutes longer. Transfer this to the mixing bowl with the beans and corn; let mixture cool for 10 minutes.

5. When cool, fold in pepper jack cheese, salt and pepper.

6. Lay tortillas out on a baking sheet. Brush one side of each tortilla with olive oil.

7. Turn the tortillas over and spread 1/2 cup of the bean mix over half of the tortilla; repeat until all tortillas are filled. Fold each tortilla in half. Repeat with remaining tortillas and bean mixture.

8. Heat a clean frying pan or griddle on medium-high heat. Cook each tortilla, for 3 minutes on each side, until golden brown and cheese is melted. Place finished quesadillas on a baking sheet and keep warm in the preheated oven until all quesadillas are cooked.

9. Cut into wedges and serve with salsa and sour cream.

Nutritional Info: Calories: 232 | Sodium: 578 mg | Dietary Fiber: 5.1 g | Total Fat: 9.7 g | Total Carbs: 27.6 g | Protein: 10.6 g.

Chicken Flautas with Avocado Cream

Servings: 16 | Prep Time: 20 minutes | Cook Time: 20 minutes

Get really hands on with your Victoria Cast Iron Tortilla Press! Scrumptious Chicken Flautas with Avocado Cream are just the thing to take to any party or barbecue. Quick and easy, served warm these party pleasers will soon become a new finger food favorite amongst family and friends.

Ingredients:

For the Flautas:

1 rotisserie chicken, skin removed and meat finely shredded

3 cups rapeseed oil

1 tablespoon butter

1/2 small onion, diced

1 jalapeno, diced

1 garlic clove, minced

1 teaspoon ground cumin

1/2 teaspoon cayenne pepper

1 cup pico de gallo

1 cup Monterey Jack cheese, shredded

1 lime, juiced

1/8 teaspoon sea salt

16 flour tortillas, made using Victoria Cast Iron tortilla press

2 cups shredded iceberg lettuce, for serving

Flour Tortillas:

3 1/2 cups all-purpose flour

3 tablespoons vegetable shortening, chilled

1 teaspoon sea salt

2 teaspoons baking powder

1 1/2 cup water

[please see page 31 for instructions]

For the Avocado Cream:

1 very ripe avocado, halved, pitted and flesh removed

1 (4-ounce) container sour cream

2 tablespoons fresh lime juice

1/8 teaspoon sea salt

Instructions:

1. Mash avocado in a mixing bowl. Fold in sour cream and lime juice until smooth. Add salt. Cover with plastic wrap and chill in the refrigerator until serving time.

2. Melt butter in a large frying pan on medium heat. Add onions and jalapeno. Sauté 5 minutes, or until tender. Add garlic, cumin and cayenne pepper. Cook 2 minutes until fragrant. Add chicken and pico de gallo; stir to combine. Remove from heat and stir in cheese and lime juice. Let cool slightly.

3. Preheat oven to warm. Line a baking sheet with aluminum foil.

4. Add rapeseed oil to a large pot. Heat over medium heat until a deep-frying thermometer reads 190C when inserted.

5. Lay flour tortillas out on a flat work space. Spread a heaping spoonful of chicken mix down the middle of each tortilla. Roll tortilla tightly around the filling and secure with a toothpick.

6. Grab a flauta with tongs, submerge in hot oil until firm, then release to continue cooking. Cook until golden brown, about 2 minutes, then transfer to a paper towel-lined plate.

7. Keep flautas warm in the oven on the baking sheet while you continue to cook the other flautas.
Place shredded lettuce on a serving platter. Lay flautas on bed of lettuce and serve with avocado cream on the side.

Nutritional Info: Calories: 534 | Sodium: 266 mg | Dietary Fiber 2.6 g | Total Fat: 50.6 g | Total Carbs: 14.0 g | Protein: 7.7 g.

Cinnamon-Sugar Tortilla Crisps with Pineapple Salsa

Servings: 6 | Prep Time: 10 minutes | Cook Time: 10 minutes

Ditch your traditional savory chips and salsa, and take a stroll on the sweet side of life with this amazing recipe. Cinnamon Sugar Tortilla Crisps hit the sweet spot—especially dipped in this tangy, tantalizing pineapple salsa. This one is sure to become a party pleasing favorite!

Ingredients:

2 cups pineapple, chopped and drained (if canned)

1 lime, juiced and zested

2 tablespoons fresh mint, chopped

1 teaspoon sugar substitute

1/4 teaspoon cinnamon

3 corn tortillas, cut into 24 triangles, made using Victoria Cast Iron tortilla press

5 tablespoons butter, unsalted and melted

Corn Tortillas:

2 cups masa harina

1/2 tablespoon sea salt

1 1/2 cups hot water

Sheet of plastic ziploc bag (cut in half)

[please see page 29 for instructions]

Instructions

1. Preheat oven to 400 degrees Fahrenheit.
2. Combine pineapple, lime juice and zest, mint and 1/2 teaspoon of sugar substitute in a mixing bowl. Place in the refrigerator to set.
3. Combine cinnamon and remaining sugar substitute in a separate mixing bowl.

4.   Line a baking sheet with aluminum foil. Next, line a plate or second baking sheet with paper towels.

5.   Brush tortilla triangles generously with melted butter and lay in a single layer on the aluminum foil lined baking sheet. Sprinkle with cinnamon sugar.

6.   Bake tortillas for 5 minutes or until golden browned. Transfer chips to paper towel-lined sheet to drain.
Let cool for five minutes and serve with pineapple salsa on the side!

Nutritional Info: Calories: 216 | Sodium: 112 mg | Dietary Fiber: 2.8 g | Total Fat: 15.1g | Total Carbs: 21.2 g | Protein: 1.8 g.

Corn and Cheese Enchiladas

Servings: 4 | Prep Time: 10 minutes | Cook Time: 20 minutes

If quick and easy meals are your thing, then this will surely become a family favorite! Corn and cheese enchiladas are budget friendly, without sacrificing that traditional Mexican flavor you love so dear. Whip some up with a side of Mexican rice for a super weeknight supper.

Ingredients:

8 corn tortillas, made using Victoria Cast Iron tortilla press

2 tablespoons olive oil

5 scallions, white and light green parts, chopped

2 shallots, finely chopped

2 medium ears of corn, husked and corn kernels removed

1/2 cup 2% ultra-filtered milk

1 teaspoon sea salt

2 cups monterey jack cheese, shredded

2 cups enchilada sauce

Corn Tortillas:

1 cup masa harina

1 teaspoon sea salt

1 cup hot water

Sheet of plastic ziploc bag (cut in half)

[please see page 29 for instructions]

Instructions

1. Pre-heat oven to 350 degrees Fahrenheit. Stack tortillas, wrap in foil and bake for 8, or until softened.

2. While tortillas are baking, oil a 7 x 11-inch glass baking dish or roasting pan with 1 tablespoon oil.

3. Heat remaining oil in large frying pan on medium-high heat.

4. Add scallions and shallots. Cook for 3-5 minutes; until fragrant. Stir in corn and milk. Cook for 7 minutes, stirring occasionally, until thickened. Fold in salt.

5. Remove tortillas from the oven. Set aside 1 cup of cheese. Spoon a heaping tablespoon of corn mixture into the center of a tortilla. Add a heaping tablespoon of cheese on top. Roll up tortilla and set in baking dish, seam side down. Repeat with remaining tortillas, overlapping them slightly.

6. Pour enchilada sauce over tortillas and cover with reserved cheese. Bake for 20 minutes, or until cheese begins to bubble.

Nutritional Info: Calories: 485 | Sodium: 819 mg | Dietary Fiber: 9.6 g | Total Fat: 27.1 g | Total Carbs: 46.7 g | Protein: 21.3 g.

Crunchy Snickerdoodle Wraps

Servings: 8 | Prep Time: 5 minutes | Cook Time: 10 minutes

Snicker doodle cookie lovers will go head over heels for these Crunchy Snickerdoodle Wraps! Ooey, gooey and creamy center with a light crunchy sweet outside—these desserts are great to pack in lunches too!

Ingredients:

8 flour tortillas, made using Victoria Cast Iron tortilla press

1 package neufchatel cheese, softened

1/2 cup sugar or 1/4 cup sugar substitute

1 tablespoon cinnamon

2 cups rapeseed oil

Flour Tortillas:

2 cups all-purpose flour

4 1/2 teaspoons vegetable shortening, chilled

1/2 teaspoon sea salt

1 teaspoon baking powder

2/3 cups water

Sheet of plastic ziploc bag (cut in half)

[please see page 31 for instructions]

Instructions:

1. Spread flour tortillas with a layer of neufchatel. Roll up tortillas and secure each with a toothpick.

2. Heat 1 inch of oil on medium high until a candy thermometer reads 175 degrees Celsius. Fry wraps until golden brown; about 3-5 minutes on both sides.

3. Transfer to a paper towel lined plate and let cool 15 seconds.

4. Combine cinnamon and sugar in a shallow dish.

5.   Roll the wraps in the cinnamon sugar and serve.

Nutritional Info: Calories: 797 | Sodium: 67 mg | Dietary Fiber 2.1 g | Total Fat: 76.7 g | Total Carbs: 28.7 g | Protein: 2.8 g.

Guacamole Volcano

Servings: 4 | Prep Time: 10 minutes | Cook Time: 15 minutes

Get fun and creative with your fresh Victoria Cast Iron tortillas and build Guacamole Volcanoes. Bursting with flavor, these scrumptious mounds of Mexican goodness will surely hit the spot.

Ingredients:

Cooking spray

4 corn tortillas, made using Victoria Cast Iron tortilla press

1 cup guacamole

2 cups warm taco seasoned beef

2 cups cheddar cheese, shredded

2 cups iceberg lettuce, finely shredded

1 tablespoon cilantro, chopped

Salsa, for garnish

Sour cream, for garnish

Corn Tortillas:

1/2 cup masa harina

1/2 teaspoon sea salt

1/2 cup hot water

Sheet of plastic ziploc bag (cut in half)

[please see page 29 for instructions]

Instructions:

1. Heat a large skillet over high heat. Spray with a thin film of cooking spray. Cook tortillas for 1 minute on both sides until blistered and soft. Transfer each to a plate.

2. Top each tortilla with 2 tablespoons guacamole. Mound 1/2 cup taco meat filling on each tortilla. Top each with 1/4 of the cheddar cheese, 1/4 of the lettuce, then the remaining guacamole, and 1/2 teaspoon of the cilantro.

3.   Serve immediately with a side of salsa and sour cream.

Nutritional Info: Calories: 134 | Sodium: 162 mg | Dietary Fiber 2.8 g | Total Fat: 8.0 g | Total Carbs: 13.5 g | Protein: 3.8 g.

Hoisin Wraps

Servings: 3 | Prep Time: 5 minutes | Cook Time: 5 minutes

A slightly spice East Asian twist on barbecue sauce, hoisin makes the perfect treat when it comes to using fresh pressed tortillas to create yummy wraps. Super-filling, hoisin wraps are great served alongside yucca fries, sweet potato fries or an ice-cold pitcher of tea.

Ingredients:

2 cups rotisserie chicken, shredded

4 tablespoons hoisin sauce

3 flour tortillas, made using Victoria Cast Iron tortilla press

1/2 cucumber, deseeded and shredded

2 spring onions, trimmed and finely shredded

1/4 cup watercress

Flour Tortillas

1 cup all-purpose flour

3 teaspoons vegetable shortening, chilled

1/4 teaspoon sea salt

1/2 teaspoon baking powder

1/2 cup water

Sheet of plastic ziploc bag (cut in half)

[please see page 31 for instructions]

Instructions:

1. Heat a grill pan to high. Mix the chicken with half of the hoisin sauce; coat well. Spread it over the grill and cook through until sizzling.

2. Wrap the tortillas in paper towels and warm them in a microwave for 15 seconds.

3. Lay the tortillas on a flat work surface. Spread the rest of the hoisin sauce evenly onto the tortillas. Spread chicken evenly down the middle of each tortilla.
4. Top with cucumber, onions and watercress.
5. Roll up like a burrito. Cut in half and enjoy while swarm.

Nutritional Info: Calories: 93 | Sodium: 329 mg | Dietary Fiber 1.1 g | Total Fat: 0.9 g | Total Carbs: 10.4 g | Protein: 11.2 g.

Hot Diggedy Dogs

Servings: 5 | Prep Time: 15 minutes | Cook Time: 25 minutes

Get ready for some tortilla fun! Hot Diggedy Dogs can be made on the grill too, for all you grill masters out there. Simply stuff these dogs in fresh tortillas and top with your favorite condiments for one super-fun meal.

Ingredients:

1 package bratwurst or uncured hot dogs

1 medium onion, thinly sliced

1 red bell pepper thinly sliced

Cooking spray

1 cup mozzarella cheese, shredded

5 corn tortillas, made using Victoria Cast Iron tortilla press

Ketchup, for garnish

Yellow mustard, for garnish

Corn Tortillas:

1/2 cup masa harina

1/2 teaspoon sea salt

1/2 cup hot water

Sheet of plastic ziploc bag (cut in half)

[please see page 29 for instructions]

Instructions:

1. Spray a medium frying pan with cooking spray. Heat on medium heat. Add bell pepper and onion. Cook until tender and slightly charred; stirring often.

2. Cook the bratwurst or hot dogs to the directions on the package.

3. Warm the tortillas in a microwave for 15 seconds.

4. Place a brat or dog in the middle of each tortilla. Top cheese, then with onion and peppers.

5.   Garnish with ketchup, mustard or your favorite condiment. Fold the tortilla over. Wrap with paper towel and enjoy!

Nutritional Info: Calories: 114 | Sodium: 235 mg | Dietary Fiber 0.8 g | Total Fat: 7.5 g | Total Carbs: 4.0 g | Protein: 7.7 g.

Margherita Tortilla Pizzas

Servings: 4 | Prep Time: 5 minutes | Cook Time: 20 minutes

When you are craving delicious, simple margherita pizzas why not turn your tortillas into something Italian! These fresh, Italian inspired pizzas will have your taste buds exploding with comfort-filled flavor right at home. Don't be afraid to explore other topping options to turn your pizza into a family fun night!

Ingredients:

4 corn or flour tortillas, made using Victoria Cast Iron tortilla press

2 tablespoons olive oil

1 cup marinara sauce

1 1/2 cups grated mozzarella cheese

Fresh basil leaves, for garnish

Corn Tortillas:

2 cups masa harina

1/2 tablespoon sea salt

1 1/2 cups hot water

Sheet of plastic ziploc bag (cut in half)

[please see page 29 for instructions]

Flour Tortillas:

1 cup all-purpose flour

3 teaspoons vegetable shortening, chilled

1/4 teaspoon sea salt

1/2 teaspoon baking powder

1/2 cup water

[please see page 31 for instructions]

Instructions:

1. Preheat the oven to 425 degrees Fahrenheit.
2. Brush each tortilla, with olive oil, on both sides.
3. Line a baking sheet with aluminum foil.
4. Bake the tortillas for 5 to 7 minutes. Remove from oven and flip tortillas.
5. Bake again for 5 to 7 minutes until they begin to turn golden brown.
6. Top each tortilla with a tablespoon or two of marinara sauce. Sprinkle with a generous amount of mozzarella cheese.
7. Place the baking sheet back into the oven and bake 7 to 9 minutes; until the cheese is melted and bubbly.
8. Garnish with a leaf or two of fresh basil.

Nutritional Info: Calories: 287 | Sodium: 522 mg | Dietary Fiber: 3.1 g | Total Fat: 16.9 g | Total Carbs: 20.8 g | Protein: 14.5 g.

Mexican Lasagna

Servings: 6-8 | Prep Time: 15 minutes | Cook Time: 35 minutes

Family fun night has never tasted so good! A light alternative to the traditional Italian dish, Mexican Lasagna is sure to spice up any night in with family and friends. Serve it up with a garden salad and cinnamon-sugar tortilla chips for one killer meal.

Ingredients:

- 2 teaspoons olive oil
- 1-pound ground beef
- 1 onion, diced
- 1 (6-ounce) can tomato paste
- 1 (15-ounce) can diced tomatoes
- 1 (15-ounce) can black beans, drained and rinsed
- 3 cups Mexican cheese, shredded
- 4 corn tortillas, made using Victoria Cast Iron tortilla press
- 1 tablespoon chili powder

- 2 teaspoons cumin
- 1 teaspoon oregano
- 1/4 teaspoon sea salt
- 1/4 teaspoon pepper
- 2 tablespoons black olives, sliced for garnish
- 2 tablespoons cilantro, chopped for garnish
- Avocados, diced for garnish
- Salsa
- Sour cream

Corn Tortillas:

- 1/2 cup masa harina
- 1/2 teaspoon sea salt
- 1/2 cup hot water

- Sheet of plastic ziploc bag (cut in half)
- [please see page 29 for instructions]

Instructions:

1. Pre-heat oven to 350 degrees Fahrenheit. Grease a 9x13 baking dish with 2 teaspoons olive oil and a paper towel; set aside.

2. Heat a large frying pan on medium-high heat. Add onion and ground beef. Cook until brown and drain grease.

3. Return frying pan to burner. Add tomato paste and diced tomatoes. Stir until well-blended. Reduce heat to medium and cook for five minutes.

4. Fold chili powder, cumin, oregano, sea salt and pepper into mixture.

5. Lay two tortillas, side by side in the bottom of the greased pan. Top with half of the meat mixture. Top meat with half the can of beans, and top beans with 2 cups of cheese. Top with two more tortillas and repeat layering process.

6. Bake at 30 minutes, until cheese is golden and bubbly. Remove from oven and let stand for five minutes before serving.

7. Top with black olives, cilantro and avocado. Serve with a side of sour cream and salsa.

Nutritional Info: Calories: 667 | Sodium: 734 mg | Dietary Fiber: 11.2 g | Total Fat: 33.9 g | Total Carbs: 50.0 g | Protein: 49.4 g.

Migas (Tex-Mex Style)

Servings: 6 | Prep Time: 5 minutes | Cook Time: 10 minutes

Spice things up for breakfast and serve up some Migas, Tex Mex Style, for something hearty and filling. You'll rule the day with the healthy energy packed in this delicious recipe. Don't forget to warm up some extra tortillas to scoop this tasty meal off your plate in true Tex-Mex Style!

Ingredients:

1/4 cup olive oil

6 corn tortillas, made using Victoria Cast Iron tortilla press

1 small onion, chopped

1 red bell pepper, diced

1 serrano pepper, diced

2 cloves garlic, minced

2 cups cherry tomatoes, halved

12 large eggs

1/4 cup ultra-filtered milk

1/2 teaspoon sea salt

3/4 cups shredded monterrey jack cheese

2 teaspoons cilantro, chopped

1/2 cup avocado, diced

1/2 cup fresh salsa

6 lime wedges

1 can refried beans

Corn Tortillas:

2 cups masa harina

1/2 tablespoon sea salt

1 1/2 cups hot water

Sheet of plastic ziploc bag (cut in half)

[please see page 29 for instructions]

Instructions

1. Heat olive oil in a large frying pan over medium-high heat.

2. Fry tortillas one at a time, 30 seconds per side, until crisp and golden.
3. Place tortillas on a paper towel lined plate covered cool.
4. Chop cooked tortillas into 1 inch squares and set aside.
5. Drain the excess oil from the pan. Return the pan to medium-high heat.
6. Add the onion, bell pepper, and serrano pepper. Sauté for five minutes, stirring often until the onion begins to caramelize and turn golden.
7. Add the garlic and tomatoes to the frying pan and cook for 3 minutes, and reduce the heat to medium low.
8. Open refried beans and warm them in a sauce pan on medium low. If they begin to dry out, add a few teaspoons of warm water and stir vigorously.
9. Combine eggs, milk and salt in a large mixing bowl with a whisk.
10. Stir in one 1/2 cup of the shredded cheese and 1 teaspoon cilantro.
11. Add the egg mix to the frying pan and cook for one minute without stirring.
12. Add the chopped tortilla chips, stirring gently to combine. Add the remaining cheese and cook until eggs are no longer runny.
13. Remove from heat and distribute evenly onto plates. Top with additional cilantro, avocado, salsa, a spoonful of refried beans and a lime wedge.

Nutritional Info: Calories: 411 | Sodium: 561 mg | Dietary Fiber: 6.5 g | Total Fat: 26.7 g | Total Carbs: 27.9 g | Protein: 20.2 g.

Mini Pizzas

Servings: 4 | Prep Time: 10 minutes | Cook Time: 15 minutes

When you're craving ooey gooey pizza with melted cheese, this is the recipe for you! Quick, simple and easy—you can turn into lunch or dinner into family fun with this delicious pizza recipe.

Ingredients:

4 flour tortillas, made using Victoria Cast Iron tortilla press

2 tablespoons olive oil

1 (15-ounce) can pizza sauce

3/4 cups mozzarella cheese, shredded

1/4 cup parmesan cheese

1 teaspoon oregano

1 teaspoon garlic powder

1 package mini turkey pepperoni

Flour Tortillas:

1 cup all-purpose flour

3 teaspoons vegetable shortening, chilled

1/4 teaspoon sea salt

1/2 teaspoon baking powder

1/2 cup water

sheet of plastic ziploc bag (cut in half)

[please see page 31 for instructions]

Instructions:

1. Preheat the oven to 425 degrees Fahrenheit.
2. Brush the inner surface of four ramekins with olive oil.
3. Warm the tortillas in a microwave for 10 seconds.

4. Gently press one tortilla into each ramekin; fold the sides over slightly taking care not to tear the tortilla.

5. Spoon 3 tablespoons of pizza sauce into each tortilla cup. Fill each cup up with mozarella. Top with parmesan cheese, a sprinkle of oregano and garlic powder.

6. Top each cup with the desired amount of turkey pepperonis.

7. Bake for 15 minutes, or until the pepperonis begin to crisp and cheese is melted.

Nutritional Info: Calories: 407 | Sodium: 1091 mg | Dietary Fiber: 3.5 g | Total Fat: 26.2 g | Total Carbs: 25.1 g | Protein: 19.5 g.

Quesadillas Rancheros

Servings: 4 | Prep Time: 15 minutes | Cook Time: 15 minutes

Spice your quesadillas up a bit and go totally rancheros style for one amazing treat! Quesadillas Rancheros are a perfect addition to any brunch with grapefruit mimosas, as an after school snack for a high protein kick, or as a comforting bite to eat to share with loved ones.

Ingredients:

8 flour tortillas, made using Victoria Cast Iron tortilla press

3 tablespoons olive oil, reserve one tablespoon for frying eggs

3 cups cheddar cheese, grated

4 large eggs

1/2 cup chorizo, diced

1 (16-ounce) can refried beans

Salsa verde, for garnish

Sliced scallions, for garnish

Hot sauce, for garnish

Flour Tortillas:

2 cups all-purpose flour

4 1/2 teaspoon vegetable shortening, chilled

1/2 teaspoon sea salt

1 teaspoon baking powder

2/3 cups water

sheet of plastic ziploc bag (cut in half)

[please see page 31 for instructions]

Instructions:

1. Pre-heat an oven to broil.
2. Line baking sheet with aluminum foil.
3. Brush all of the tortillas, on one side, with olive oil and flip to fill.

4. Spread refried beans on one side of each tortilla. Top beans with a tablespoon or two of chorizo. Cover each half with cheese. Fold each tortilla in half and transfer to foil lined baking sheet.

5. Add reserved olive oil to a frying pan on medium heat. Fry all four eggs, sunny side up until white is solid and no longer runny.

6. Broil the quesadillas for 1 to 2 minutes per side; until cheese is melted.

7. Top each quesadilla with one egg.

8. Garnish with salsa, scallions, and hot sauce. Serve piping hot!

Nutritional Info: Calories: 843 | Sodium: 1307 mg | Dietary Fiber: 9.0 g | Total Fat: 57.2 g | Total Carbs: 41.0 g | Protein: 43.2 g.

Queso Fundido con Chorizo

Servings: 10 | Prep Time: 10 minutes | Cook Time: 20 minutes

Looking for a fun, easy dip to add to your favorite party!? Queso Fundido con Chorizo is so easy—the kids can help out. This spicy treat is sure to liven up any party or rainy day. Simply serve with fresh tortilla chips and let the fun begin!

Ingredients:

- 4 ounces fresh chorizo, casings removed and crumbled
- 1 tablespoon olive oil
- 1 small red onion, chopped
- 1 clove garlic, minced
- 5 teaspoons plain flour
- 1/2 cup mexican lager, such as Negra Modelo
- 1/4 cup pickled jalapeno, chopped
- 1 tablespoon jalapeno pickling juice
- 3/4 cups ultra-filtered milk
- 2 cups monterey jack cheese, finely diced
- 2 cups whole-milk mozzarella, finely diced
- 2 tablespoons cilantro, chopped
- Tortilla chips, for dipping [see baked tortilla chips recipe for instructions]

Corn Tortillas:

- 1/2 cup masa harina
- 1/2 teaspoon sea salt
- 1/2 cup hot water
- Sheet of plastic ziploc bag (cut in half)
- [please see page 29 for instructions]

Instructions:

1. Heat a medium frying pan over medium-high heat. Add chorizo. Cook until golden, about 5 minutes.

2. Drain and transfer to paper towel lined plate.

3. Reduce the heat to medium and add the olive oil. Add the onions, stirring occasionally, until soft, 5 to 6 minutes.

4. Add the garlic and cook, stirring, until fragrant, about 30 seconds.

5. Sprinkle in the flour and cook, stirring for 1 minute, until the flour is golden.

6. Whisk in the beer and bring to a boil.

7. Stir in the chopped jalapenos and pickling juice and cook for 2 minutes.

8. Gradually add the milk, whisking, and bring back to a gentle boil and cook until thickened, about 1 minute.

9. Add the cheeses and reduce to low heat. Cook for 3 minutes, stirring frequently, until the cheese fully melts. Fold in the chorizo.

10. Transfer to a serving dish, garnish with the cilantro and serve with fresh homemade tortilla chips.

Nutritional Info: Calories: 236.7 | Sodium: 406 mg | Dietary Fiber 0 g | Total Fat: 17.0 g | Total Carbs: 4.1 g | Protein: 15.8 g.

Salami and Roasted Red Pepper Wraps

Servings: 4 | Prep Time: 15 minutes | Cook Time: 15 minutes

Craving something sweet and spicy!? This scrumptious salami and roasted red pepper wraps will totally hit the spot. Great for lunch, dinner or an afternoon snack—these wraps go perfect with a pitcher of Sangria too!

Ingredients:

4 cups shredded romaine lettuce

1 cup roasted red peppers, diced

1/2 cup and 2 tablespoons olive oil

2 tablespoons apple cider vinegar

1/2 teaspoon sugar substitute

1/2 teaspoon garlic powder

8 ounces sliced salami

1/2 cup cream cheese

1 teaspoon coarse ground black pepper

4 flour tortillas, made using Victoria Cast Iron tortilla press

Flour Tortillas:

1 cup all-purpose flour

3 teaspoons vegetable shortening, chilled

1/4 teaspoon sea salt

1/2 teaspoon baking powder

1/2 cup water

Sheet of plastic ziploc bag (cut in half)

[please see page 31 for instructions]

Instructions:

1. Toss the lettuce, roasted red peppers, olive oil, apple cider vinegar, sugar substitute and garlic powder in a large mixing bowl until well coated.

2.   Lay the tortillas on a flat surface. Spread each with an even layer of cream cheese. Sprinkle a pinch of black pepper onto cream cheese.

3.   Top cream cheese with an even layer of salami. Add two tablespoons of red pepper mix, and roll up.

4.   Serve with your favorite veggie chips or carrot sticks.

Nutritional Info: Calories: 543 | Sodium: 856 mg | Dietary Fiber: 2.6 g | Total Fat: 48.8 g | Total Carbs: 18.2 g | Protein: 11.5 g.

Salsa and Chips

Yield: 6 servings: 6 | Prep Time: 1 hour 20 minutes | Cook Time: 32 minutes

Snack super-healthy with your Victoria Cast Iron Tortilla Press! Nothing beats classic salsa and chips. Made right in the comfort of your own home, you'll love keeping this delicious salsa and chips on hand for after-school snacks or movie nights in!

Ingredients:

For the Salsa:

4 ripe tomatoes, cored and diced

1/2 medium onion, chopped

1 jalapeno, seeded and minced

1/4 cup cilantro, chopped

1/2 teaspoon sugar substitute

For the Tortilla Chips:

20 corn tortillas, cut into triangles

2 cups rapeseed oil

1 teaspoon chili powder

1 teaspoon cumin powder

1 teaspoon paprika

1 teaspoon fine salt

Corn Tortillas:

2 cups masa harina

1 1/2 teaspoons sea salt

1 1/2 cups hot water

Sheet of plastic ziploc bag (cut in half)

[please see page 29 for instructions]

Instructions:

1. Combine tomatoes, onion, jalapeno, cilantro and sugar substitute in a mixing bowl. Cover with plastic wrap and set aside for 1 hour. Serve with tortilla chips.

2. Mix chili powder, cumin powder, paprika and salt in a bowl. Set aside.

3. Pour the oil into a large heavy-bottomed pot. Place a deep-frying thermometer into the pot. Heat the oil over medium heat to 182°C.

4. Raise the heat to high. Working in small batches, fry the chips for 2 minutes, turning them with a skimmer or slotted spoon, until golden brown.

5. Transfer the chips to a paper towel-lined plate to drain.

6. Return the oil to the proper temperature between batches.

7. Dust tortilla chips with chili season mix. Serve with fresh salsa.

Nutritional Info: Calories: 214 | Sodium: 628 mg | Dietary Fiber 6.9 g | Total Fat: 5.0 g | Total Carbs: 39.8 g | Protein: 5.6 g.

Spiced Tortilla Crisps with Hummus

Servings: 4 | Prep Time: 10 minutes | Cook Time: 6 minutes

Serve up fresh, spiced tortilla crisps with your favorite hummus. A nutritious healthy snack, this recipe is sure to tide cravings between meals so you can keep the weight down. Make it a crudité plate and serve this recipe up with carrot, red pepper and cucumber sticks.

Ingredients:

4 corn tortillas, cut into 2-inch strips; made using Victoria Cast Iron tortilla press

1/3 cup and 2 tablespoons olive oil

1 teaspoon sesame seeds

1 teaspoon chili powder

1 teaspoon cumin

2 teaspoons paprika

1 teaspoon sea salt

1 teaspoon black pepper

1 (5-ounce) package hummus

Corn Tortillas:

2 cups masa harina

1/2 tablespoon sea salt

1 1/2 cups hot water

Sheet of plastic ziploc bag (cut in half)

[please see page 29 for instructions]

Instructions:

1. Pre-heat an oven to 425 degrees Fahrenheit.
2. Toss the tortilla strips with the 1/3 cup olive oil, sesame seeds, chili powder, cumin, sea salt and 1 teaspoon paprika in a large metal mixing bowl.
3. Transfer seasoned tortilla strips to two baking sheets in one single layer.

4.   Bake for 3 minutes. Swap racks with the baking sheets. Bake for 3 additional minutes until tortilla strips are golden crisp.

5.   Drizzle your hummus with 2 tablespoons olive oil and sprinkled with the remaining teaspoon of paprika and black pepper.

Nutritional Info: Calories: 268 | Sodium: 621 mg | Dietary Fiber: 4.5 g | Total Fat: 21.6 g | Total Carbs: 17.5 g | Protein: 4.5 g.

Spicy Vegetable Chapati Wraps

Servings: 3 | Prep Time: 10 minutes | Cook Time: 20 minutes

If you like chapati, you'll love these amazing Spicy Vegetable Chapati Wraps. These tantalizingly warm wraps filled with spices from the Far East, will warm your healthy soul. Serve with chai tea for one sincerely sweet experience!

Ingredients:

1 cup sweet potato, peeled and cubed

1 (15-ounce) can petite diced tomatoes

1 (15-ounce) can chickpeas, rinsed and drained

1/2 teaspoon red pepper flakes

1 tablespoon mild curry paste

1/4 cup baby spinach leaves

1 tablespoon cilantro, chopped

3 flour tortillas, made using Victoria Cast Iron tortilla press

2 tablespoons fat-free Greek yogurt, plain

Flour Tortillas:

1 cup all-purpose flour

3 teaspoons vegetable shortening, chilled

1/4 teaspoon sea salt

1/2 teaspoon baking powder

1/2 cup water

Sheet of plastic ziploc bag (cut in half)

[please see page 31 for instructions]

Instructions:

1. Cook the sweet potatoes in a pot of boiling water for 10-12 minutes until tender.

2. Combine tomatoes, chickpeas, chili flakes and curry paste in another pan and simmer gently for about 5 minutes.

3. Preheat a grill or grill pan on medium heat.

4. Drain the sweet potatoes and add to the tomato mixture. Stir in the spinach and cilantro. Cook for 1 minute until it begins to wilt.

5. Sprinkle the tortillas with a little water and grill for 20-30 seconds on each side.

6. Spoon the filling down the middle of each tortilla. Top with yogurt and fold in half to serve.

Nutritional Info: Calories: 990 | Sodium: 119 mg | Dietary Fiber 45.0 g | Total Fat: 16.1 g |
Total Carbs: 171.1 g | Protein: 48.2 g.

Tabasco Quesadillas

Servings: 4 | Prep Time: 25 minutes | Cook Time: 10 minutes

Serve up something "hot, hot, hot" with these fiery Tabasco Quesadillas. Paired with mango salsa for a cool, tangy twist—these quesadillas are absolutely delicious. Great for a meal with friends, serve your freshly pressed Tabasco Quesadillas with a bucket of Mexican cerveza and bring the party right to your home.

Ingredients:

1 tablespoon olive oil

8 flour tortillas, made using Victoria Cast Iron tortilla press

2 cups monterey jack cheese, shredded

1 spring onion, finely chopped

Tabasco® sauce

1 cup guacamole

Flour Tortillas:

3 1/2 cups all-purpose flour

3 tablespoons vegetable shortening, chilled

1 teaspoon sea salt

2 teaspoons baking powder

1 1/2 cups water

[please see page 31 for instructions]

For the Mango Salsa:

2 medium ripe mangos, skinned stoned and diced

1 red onion, diced

3 tablespoons cilantro, chopped

3 teaspoons tabasco® sauce

1 lime, juiced

1/4 teaspoon sugar substitute

Instructions:

1. Combine mango salsa ingredients together in a mixing bowl. Cover with plastic wrap and place in the refrigerator to set.

2. Wipe the base of a large frying pan with olive oil using a paper towel. Heat on medium-high.

3. Place a tortilla in frying pan and scatter over a few spring onions. Add a generous amount of tabasco® sauce in between the spring onions over the surface of the tortilla. Top with a generous layer of cheese. Continue to heat until the cheese starts to melt.

4. Place a second tortilla over the cheesy layer and press down. Flip over and continue to cook the tortilla until golden crisp. Repeat until all tortillas are finished.

5. Serve with a side of guacamole and mango salsa.

Nutritional Info: Calories: 472 | Sodium: 380 mg | Dietary Fiber 7.0 g | Total Fat: 24.4 g | Total Carbs: 49.0 g | Protein: 18.0 g.

Taco Salad in Tortilla Bowl

Servings: 4 | Prep Time: 10 minutes | Cook Time: 16 minutes

Bring the taste of delicious restaurant style Mexican food right to the comfort of your own kitchen. The best part about these delectable little taco bowls—you can prep them for the week ahead, and keep them in an airtight container for 2-3 days, for a delicious lunch option at school or work.

Ingredients:

For the tortilla Bowls:

Olive oil cooking spray

4 flour tortillas, made using Victoria Cast Iron tortilla press

For the Taco salad:

1 head iceberg lettuce, shredded

1 (15-ounce) black beans, drained and rinsed

2 cups cheddar cheese, shredded

1/2 cup sour cream

1/2 cup pico de gallo

1 cup avocado, diced

Flour Tortillas:

1 cup all-purpose flour

3 teaspoons vegetable shortening, chilled

1/4 teaspoon sea salt

1/2 teaspoon baking powder

1/2 cup water

Sheet of plastic ziploc bag (cut in half)

[please see page 31 for instructions]

Instructions:

1. Pre-heat oven to 375 degrees Fahrenheit.

2. Coat the inside of 4 oven safe bowls with cooking spray.

3. Gently press a tortilla inside each bowl.

4. Place bowls on two large baking sheets. Bake for 14-16 minutes or until evenly browned. Remove tortilla bowls and set aside to cool for 5 minutes before transferring to wire cooling rack.

5. Fill each bowl with 1/2 cup of lettuce, some black beans, shredded cheese, a dollop of sour cream, pico de gallo and avocado.

Nutritional Info: Calories: 703 | Sodium: 627 mg | Dietary Fiber 14.2 g | Total Fat: 35.6 g |
Total Carbs: 61.1 g | Protein: 36.8 g.

Tortilla Wrapped Hot Dogs

Servings: 8 | Prep Time: 15 minutes | Cook Time: 15 minutes

Spice up your party food with these super easy Tortilla Wrapped Hot Dogs. Fun for all ages, these delicious dogs wrapped with fresh tortillas are just the right amount of comfort food meets party. Serve them up with a spicy queso fundido or simply dip these dogs in classic ketchup and mustard for a tasty treat.

Ingredients:

8 corn tortillas, made using Victoria Cast Iron tortilla press

8 uncured turkey dogs, like Oscar Mayer Selects

2/3 cup olive oil

1 (10-ounce) can of tomatoes with green chiles, like RoTel

2 cups high melting point cheese, like Velveeta or Asadero

Toothpicks, for securing wraps

Corn Tortillas:

1 cup masa harina

1 teaspoon sea salt

1 cup hot water

Sheet of plastic ziploc bag (cut in half)

[please see page 29 for instructions]

Instructions:

1. Add cheese to a saucepan or crock pot and warm on medium-low heat. When cheese begins to melt, fold in tomato chili mix. Stir well to blend. Turn heat to warm.

2. Wrap tortillas in a paper towel. Place on a microwave safe plate. Warm in the microwave for five seconds. Flip tortillas and warm again for an additional five seconds.

3. Heat 2/3 cups olive oil in a frying pan on medium-high heat.

4. Wrap tortillas around turkey dogs and secure with a toothpick. Leave hot dogs whole or slice them into fours to form tortilla dog bites.

5. Place the wrapped hot dogs into the heated oil and fry until the tortilla is golden crisp, turning once, about 5 minutes per side. Transfer hot dogs to a paper towel lined plate to drain excess oil.

6. Give the queso fundido a good stir. Transfer queso to a serving bowl for kids or keep on warm for parties; and serve!

Nutritional Info: Calories: 486 | Sodium: 973 mg | Dietary Fiber: 2.1 g | Total Fat: 38.5 g | Total Carbs: 21.5 g | Protein: 18.1 g.

10

Lunch or Dinner "On the Go"

Achaari Salmon Wraps

Servings: 2 | Prep Time: 10 minutes | Cook Time: 10-15 minutes

Warm up your taste buds with something sweet and spicy! Achaari Salmon Wraps are the perfect meal for those who need a good dose of healthy fats, vegetables and antioxidants. Quick and easy, this is sure to become a family favorite in no time.

Ingredients

2 tablespoons olive oil

5 ounces salmon, skin removed and cut into 1-inch pieces

1/3 cup frozen carrots, diced

1/4 cup sweet onion, diced

1/2 cup green pepper, diced

1/4 red pepper, diced

1/4 cup yellow pepper, diced

2 kaffir lime leaves

1/4 teaspoon red chili flakes

1 jar tikka masala curry sauce, like Sherwood's or Patak's

2 tablespoons cilantro, chopped

4 corn tortillas, made using Victoria Cast Iron tortilla press

Corn Tortillas:

1/2 cup masa harina

1/2 teaspoon sea salt

1/2 cup hot water

Sheet of plastic ziploc bag (cut in half)

[please see page 29 for instructions]

Instructions

1. Heat the olive oil on medium-high heat in a wok. Fry the carrot, onion and peppers for three minutes until softened. Add the salmon and fry for two minutes.

159

2.   Stir in the tikka masala curry sauce, kaffir lime leaves and chili flakes. Sauté for 3 minutes. Add the chopped coriander, stir to mix well, reduce heat and simmer for 5 minutes.

3.   Lay tortillas on a flat surface. Fill with the achari stir fry. Roll and serve.

Nutritional Info: Calories: 596 | Sodium: 68 mg | Dietary Fiber: 6.9 g | Total Fat: 34.8 g | Total Carbs: 51.8 g | Protein: 17.4 g.

Agustine's Beer and Tequila Carnitas

Servings: 10 | Prep Time: 3 hours | Cook Time: 1 hour 10 minutes

Beer and Tequila connoisseurs rejoice! Agustine's Beer and Tequila Carnitas combines the best of both worlds for one savory tortilla filled treat. Topped with pico de gallo, you can't go wrong with this recipe.

Ingredients:

4 pounds bone-in pork shoulder

2 cups onion, diced

4 poblano peppers, diced

2 tablespoons garlic, minced

2 teaspoons sea salt, divided

1/2 teaspoon fresh ground pepper

3 cups tomatoes, cored, diced and seeded

1 cup white tequila, like Espolon

2 (12-ounce) bottles dark Mexican beer, like Negra Modelo

20 corn tortillas, warmed, made using Victoria Cast Iron tortilla press

2 cups pico de gallo

Corn Tortillas:

2 cups masa harina

1/2 tablespoon sea salt

1 1/2 cups hot water

Sheet of plastic ziploc bag (cut in half)

[please see page 29 for instructions]

Instructions:

1. Trim enough fat from pork to yield about 1/3 cup. Cut pork into 1-inch cubes.

2. Heat a large heavy soup pot or Dutch oven over medium-low heat and add the pork fat. Cook 8-10 minutes, stirring, until there is a thin layer of fat covering the

bottom and the bits left in the pot are brown and crispy. Increase heat to medium and add onion, poblanos, garlic, 1 teaspoon salt and pepper. Cook 10 minutes, stirring, until the onion is softened.

3. Add the cubed pork and cook 10 minutes, stirring frequently, until enough liquid has been released to almost cover the pork and vegetables.

4. Reduce heat to medium-low, cover and cook for 15 minutes. Uncover, increase heat to maintain a lively simmer, and cook for 30 more minutes, stirring occasionally, until the liquid has reduced to a thick paste.

5. Stir in tomatoes, return to a simmer and continue to cook, stirring occasionally, for 10 minutes.

6. Add tequila and cook 15-20 minutes, stirring occasionally, until the liquid has evaporated and a thick sauce coats the meat. Slowly fold in the beer and return to a lively simmer. Cook 30-45 minutes more, stirring occasionally, until all the liquid has evaporated.

7. Season with the remaining 1 teaspoon salt and pepper to taste.

8. Transfer the carnitas to a serving platter. Pile carnitas in the middle of a warm tortilla and top with pico de gallo.

Nutritional Info: Calories: 760 | Sodium: 835 mg | Dietary Fiber 4.5 g | Total Fat: 40.4 g | Total Carbs: 32.0 g | Protein: 46.5 g.

Barbecue Portobello Quesadillas

Servings: 4 | Prep Time: 15 minutes | Cook Time: 45 minutes

Spice things up for dinner with these mellow Barbecue Portobello Quesadillas. One bite and you'll be transported into sweet southern comfort combined with the warm flavor of portobellos—these quesadillas might just become your new "go to" for comfort food.

Ingredients:

1/2 cup prepared barbecue sauce, like Kraft Mesquite

1 tablespoon tomato paste

1 tablespoon apple cider vinegar

1 (4-ounce) can chipotle chilies in adobo sauce, chopped

1 tablespoon plus 2 teaspoons olive oil, divided

5 medium portobello mushrooms, gills removed and diced

1 medium onion, finely diced

4 flour tortillas, made using Victoria Cast Iron tortilla press

2 cups monterey jack cheese, shredded

Flour Tortillas:

1 cup all-purpose flour

3 teaspoons vegetable shortening, chilled

1/4 teaspoon sea salt

1/2 teaspoon baking powder

1/2 cup water

Sheet of plastic ziploc bag (cut in half)

[please see page 31 for instructions]

Instructions:

1. Combine barbecue sauce, tomato paste, vinegar and 1/3 of the chopped chipotle peppers in a mixing bowl.

2. Heat 1 tablespoon oil in a large nonstick skillet over medium heat. Add mushrooms and cook for 5 minutes; stirring occasionally. Add onion and cook for 5-7 minutes. Transfer the vegetables to the bowl with the barbecue sauce; stir to combine.

3. Wipe out the pan with a paper towel.

4. Lay tortillas on a flat work surface. Spread 3 tablespoons of cheese on half of each tortilla and top with 1/2 cup of the barbecue portobello mix. Fold tortillas in half and press gently to flatten.

5. Heat 1 teaspoon oil in the pan over medium heat. Add two quesadillas and cook, turning once, until golden on both sides, 3 to 4 minutes in total.

6. Transfer to a cutting board and tent with foil to keep warm. Repeat with the remaining 1 teaspoon olive oil and quesadillas.

7. Cut each quesadilla into wedges and serve.

Nutritional Info: Calories: 371 | Sodium: 672 mg | Dietary Fiber 3.1 g | Total Fat: 21.5 g | Total Carbs: 29.2 g | Protein: 16.9 g.

Beef and Pineapple Tacos

Servings: 4 | Prep Time: 15 minutes | Cook Time: 5-10 minutes

Sweet, savory, and slightly spicy; this recipe is so simple and quick—you'll add it to your favorite dinners to whip up in less than 30 minutes. Add your favorite hot sauce for a bit of a kick, or eat it as is for those who like things a little on the mild side.

Ingredients:

1-pound steak, cut into 1-inch thin strips

1/2 teaspoon sea salt

1/2 teaspoon black pepper

1 tablespoon olive oil

2 cups pineapple, chopped

1/2 ancho chili, deseeded and sliced

8 corn tortillas, made using Victoria Cast Iron tortilla press

1/4 cup cilantro, chopped

4 lime wedges, for serving

Corn Tortillas:

1 cup masa harina

1 teaspoon sea salt

1 cup hot water

Sheet of plastic ziploc bag (cut in half)

[please see page 29 for instructions]

Instructions:

1. Heat the oil in a large frying pan over medium-high heat.
2. Season the steak with salt and pepper.
3. Heat an oven to 350 degrees Fahrenheit. Wrap tortillas in aluminum foil.
4. Place them in the oven when up to temperature and turn the oven down to warm.

5.   Place the seasoned steak strips in the pan and cook the steak to the desired temperature; 1 to 2 minutes per side for rare, 3 minutes for medium rare and further for done.

6.   Add the pineapple and ancho chili to the frying pan and cook, stirring constantly for 6 minutes or until tender.

7.   Remove the tortillas from the oven and place flat on a plate.
Divide the steak and pineapple mix evenly across the tortillas. Top with a pinch of cilantro. Serve with a lime wedge on the side.

Nutritional Info: Calories: 405 | Sodium: 315 mg | Dietary Fiber: 4.5 g | Total Fat: 10.7 g | Total Carbs: 33.1 g | Protein: 44.3 g.

Brown Rice and Bean Burrito

Servings: 3 | Prep Time: 5 minutes | Cook Time: 10 minutes

If you're looking for a super-quick meal to take on the go, this simple Brown Rice and Bean Burrito is just the one for you. Vegetarian friendly, this delicious burrito is packed full of healthy nutrients, lean protein and heart healthy carbs. Enjoy it with a cold glass of water to stay hydrated and full all day long.

Ingredients:

1/4 cup brown rice, cooked

1 tablespoon cheddar cheese, shredded

1/4 avocado

1 teaspoon fresh lime juice

3 flour tortillas, made using Victoria Cast Iron tortilla press

2 tablespoons no-salt-added canned black beans

1 tablespoon salsa

2 tablespoons sour cream

Flour Tortillas:

1 cup all-purpose flour

3 teaspoons vegetable shortening, chilled

1/4 teaspoon sea salt

1/2 teaspoon baking powder

1/2 cup water

Sheet of plastic ziploc bag (cut in half)

[please see page 31 for instructions]

Instructions:

1. Cook brown rice to package instructions. Remove from stove and fold in cheddar until it melts. Fold in beans and set aside to cool to room temperature.

2. Mash the avocado and lime juice together in a small bowl with a fork until smooth. Fold in salsa.

3. Lay the tortilla on a flat work surface. Spread the mashed avocado mix across the tortilla. Spread the cheesy rice mix down the middle of the tortilla.

4. Roll over once then tightly tuck in the sides and continue rolling. Cut in half.

5. Wrap in a paper towel, followed by a layer of aluminum foil. Serve at room temperature.

Nutritional Info: Calories: 496 | Sodium: 170 mg | Dietary Fiber 10.5 g | Total Fat: 19.5 g | Total Carbs: 69.2 g | Protein: 13.9 g.

Carrot and Hummus Roll-Ups

Servings: 3 | Prep Time: 10 minutes | Cook Time: 10 minute

Packed lunch has never tasted so good! Spice up your lunchtime with these sweet and spicy Carrot and Hummus Roll-ups. Super quick and easy, you can prep them the night before for any outing, to take to work, or to simply just grab and go!

Ingredients:

1 tub of roasted red pepper hummus

1 teaspoon paprika

1 teaspoon olive oil

1/4 teaspoon salt

1/4 teaspoon pepper

3 flour tortillas, made using Victoria Cast Iron tortilla press

4 carrots, shredded

Flour Tortillas:

1 cup all-purpose flour

3 teaspoons vegetable shortening, chilled

1/4 teaspoon sea salt

1/2 teaspoon baking powder

1/2 cup water

Sheet of plastic ziploc bag (cut in half)

[please see page 31 for instructions]

Instructions:

1. Combine hummus, paprika, olive oil, salt and pepper in a mixing bowl.
2. Spread the hummus across each tortilla.
3. Top hummus with carrots. Roll up tight and serve with a fresh garden salad.

Nutritional Info: Calories: 189 | Sodium: 550 mg | Dietary Fiber 6.5 g | Total Fat: 7.7 g | Total Carbs: 25.4 g | Protein: 3.3 g.

Chicken Fajitas

Servings: 5 | Prep Time: 25 minutes | Cook Time: 15 minutes

Make dinner night sizzle with these yummy Chicken Fajitas! Bring restaurant style grilled food right into the comfort of your own kitchen when you go bold with these delicious fajitas. Serve with homemade margaritas and make it a party with friends and family.

Ingredients:

2 tablespoons cilantro

1 lime, juiced

1/4 cup chicken stock

2 cloves garlic, minced

1 jalapeno, seeded and chopped

1 tablespoon honey

1/8 teaspoon sea salt

3 boneless skinless chicken breasts, cut into strips

1 teaspoon chili powder

1 teaspoon cumin powder

1 teaspoon garlic powder

1 onion, sliced into 1/2-inch thick rounds

1 yellow pepper, seeded and quartered

1 red pepper, seeded and quartered

1 1/2 teaspoons olive oil

10 corn tortillas, made using Victoria Cast Iron tortilla press

2 cups oaxaca cheese, grated

Salsa, for garnish

Sour cream, for garnish

Corn Tortillas:

2 cups all-purpose flour

4 1/2 teaspoons vegetable shortening, chilled

1/2 teaspoon sea salt

1 teaspoon baking powder

2/3 cups water

Sheet of plastic ziploc bag (cut in half)

[please see page 29 for instructions]

Instructions:

---

1. Add cilantro, lime juice, chicken broth, garlic, jalapeno, honey, and salt to a blender, puree until smooth.

2. Add chicken to a mixing bowl with chili powder, cumin and garlic powder. Toss to coat.

3. Add the peppers, onions. Pour blender puree into the bowl. Toss well to coat the chicken and vegetables. Let stand, at room temperature, for up to 30 minutes.

4. Heat the oil in a grill pan on medium high heat. Grill the chicken and vegetables for 5 to 8 minutes, turning, until the vegetables are tender. Remove the vegetables and continue to grill chicken for 5 to 7 more minutes; until the chicken is cooked through. Set aside.

5. Place the tortillas on the grill until just warmed through, about 30 seconds.

6. Place some peppers, onions, and chicken in a tortilla. Top with cheese, salsa and sour cream. Enjoy!

Nutritional Info: Calories: 448 | Sodium: 463 mg | Dietary Fiber 4.8 g | Total Fat: 20.8 g | Total Carbs: 32.1 g | Protein: 34.4 g.

Chicken Mushroom Quesadillas

Servings: 4 | Prep Time: 12 minutes | Cook Time: 15 minutes

Warm, earthy Chicken and Mushroom Quesadillas are healthy, indulgent and super-filling. Stuffed with lean protein and veggies, these quesadillas will definitely elevate any clean diet with fresh Victoria Cast Iron pressed tortillas. Serve them up with a side salad or homemade guacamole dip for an even more filling super healthy antioxidant boosting meal!

Ingredients:

1 teaspoon olive oil

1 medium onion, chopped

2 cups white button mushrooms

3 cloves garlic, minced

1 boneless chicken breast, chopped

1 teaspoon ground cumin

1 teaspoon chili powder

1 teaspoon dried oregano

1/4 cup baby spinach leaves, sliced

1/2 teaspoon sea salt

1/4 teaspoon coarse black pepper

1 cup cheddar cheese, shredded

4 flour tortillas, made using Victoria Cast Iron tortilla press

2 tablespoons butter, unsalted

Salsa, for garnish

Sour cream, for garnish

Flour Tortillas:

1 cups all-purpose flour

3 teaspoons vegetable shortening, chilled

1/4 teaspoon sea salt

1/2 teaspoon baking powder

1/2 cup water

Sheet of plastic ziploc bag (cut in half)

[please see page 31 for instructions]

Instructions:

1. Heat the olive oil in a large frying pan over a medium heat. Add the onions and cook for five minutes. Add the mushrooms and cook until the mushroom water is evaporated and they begin to brown, 5 to 7 minutes. Add the garlic and cook for an additional minute. Add chicken, cumin, chili powder and oregano; stir until all spices are incorporated. Add spinach, salt and pepper. Cook for two minutes, until spinach is slightly wilted.

2. Lay one tortilla on a flat work surface and sprinkle with desired amount of cheddar cheese.

3. Spoon half the chicken mix on top of cheese. Top with more cheese. Lay a flour tortilla on top. Assemble second quesadilla the same way.

4. Heat a large frying-pan with 1 tablespoon butter over medium heat. Carefully place one quesadilla in the frying pan and cook for three minutes. Gently flip quesadilla and cook for an additional three minutes, until golden brown on both sides and cheese is melted. Repeat with second quesadilla and remaining butter.

5. Slice quesadillas into quarters. Place two quarters on a plate with a side of sour cream and salsa.

Nutritional Info: Calories: 324 | Sodium: 505 mg | Dietary Fiber: 3.0 g | Total Fat: 20.1 g | Total Carbs: 16.5 g | Protein: 20.8 g.

Chilaquiles Casserole

Servings: 10 | Prep Time: 10 minutes | Cook Time: 23 minutes

If you love chilaquiles this one dish hot pot will transform family dinner at your house in a snap! Warm, mildly spicy and packed full of superfoods—this isn't your average casserole. Serve family style with salad and a pitcher of spa water for one genuinely clean, healthy meal.

Ingredients:

1 tablespoon olive oil

1 medium onion, diced

1 zucchini, peeled and grated

1 (15-ounce) can black beans, rinsed and drained

1 (15-ounce) can diced tomatoes, drained

1 1/2 cups frozen corn kernels, thawed

1 teaspoon ground cumin

1/4 teaspoon cinnamon

1/2 teaspoon salt

10 corn tortillas, quartered, made using Victoria Cast Iron tortilla press

1 (19-ounce) can mild red or green enchilada sauce

1 1/4 cups cheddar cheese, shredded

Cooking spray

Corn Tortillas:

1 cup masa harina

1 teaspoon sea salt

1 cup hot water

Sheet of plastic ziploc bag (cut in half)

[please see page 29 for instructions]

Instructions:

1.   Preheat oven to 400 degrees. Coat a 9x13-inch baking dish with cooking spray.

2. Heat olive oil in a large nonstick frying pan over medium-high heat. Add onion and cook 5 minutes, stirring often, until starting to brown. Add zucchini, beans, tomatoes, corn, cumin, cinnamon and salt. Cook 3 minutes stirring occasionally, until the vegetables are heated through.

3. Add half the tortilla pieces in the bottom of the baking dish. Top with half the vegetable mixture, half the enchilada sauce and half of the cheese. Follow with another layer of tortillas, vegetables, sauce and cheese. Cover with foil.

4. Bake the casserole for 15 minutes. Remove the foil and continue baking for an additional 10 minutes; until the casserole is bubbling around the edges and the cheese is melted. Serve hot.

Nutritional Info: Calories: 331 | Sodium: 579 mg | Dietary Fiber 10.3 g | Total Fat: 8.6 g | Total Carbs: 50.3 g | Protein: 15.9 g.

Chipotle Prawn Tacos

Servings: 5 | Prep Time: 10 minutes | Cook Time: 20 minutes

Spice things up for dinner with these fresh homemade chipotles peppered prawn tacos. Quick and easy, these tacos make for a great weeknight meal. Serve with a side of mexican rice or cinnamon sugar dusted tortilla chips for something a little sweet and savory.

Ingredients:

1 tablespoon olive oil

1 teaspoon chipotle chili powder

1 teaspoon sea salt

20 medium prawns, peeled and deveined

10 corn tortillas, made using Victoria Cast Iron tortilla press

Chopped cilantro, for garnish

1 avocado, pitted, peeled and diced

1/2 cup sour cream

1 lime juiced and zested

2 limes, cut into wedges

Corn Tortillas:

1 cup masa harina

1 teaspoon sea salt

1 cup hot water

Sheet of plastic ziploc bag (cut in half)

[please see page 29 for instructions]

Instructions:

1. Mash the avocado in a mixing bowl. Fold in sour cream, lime juice and zest. Mix until smooth.

2. Heat a grill pan to medium heat. Mix the olive oil, chipotle powder and salt in a large bowl. Add the prawns and toss to coat.

3. Grill the prawns for 2 minutes on each side until pink and firm. Transfer to a paper towel lined plate.

4. Grill the tortillas until slightly charred and pliable, about 20 seconds per side.

5. Spoon the sauce on the tortilla, then top with about 2 or 3 prawns and fresh cilantro. Serve with a lime wedge on the side.

Nutritional Info: Calories: 179 | Sodium: 314 mg | Dietary Fiber 3.2 g | Total Fat: 9.1 g | Total Carbs: 13.7 g | Protein: 12.0 g.

Crab Quesadillas

Servings: 4 | Prep Time: 30 minutes | Cook Time: 30 minutes

Stuff your quesadillas with seafood for a fresh take on tortilla fun. Another great way to cook up something fun with your fresh pressed Victoria Cast Iron Tortillas, this recipe is simply sweet with a little kick. You're sure to spice things up at any mealtime with these yummy Crab Quesadillas.

Ingredients:

1 cup cheddar cheese, shredded

2 ounces neufchatel cheese, softened

4 scallions, chopped

1/2 red bell pepper, finely chopped

1/3 cup cilantro, chopped

2 tablespoons pickled jalapenos, chopped

1 teaspoon orange zest

1 tablespoon orange juice

8 ounces crabmeat, drained if necessary

4 flour tortillas, made using Victoria Cast Iron tortilla press

2 teaspoons olive oil, divided

Flour Tortillas:

1 cup all-purpose flour

3 teaspoons vegetable shortening, chilled

1/4 teaspoon sea salt

1/2 teaspoon baking powder

1/2 cup water

Sheet of plastic ziploc bag (cut in half)

[please see page 31 for instructions]

Instructions:

1. Combine Cheddar, neufchatel, scallions, bell pepper, cilantro, jalapenos, orange zest and juice in a mixing bowl. Gently fold in crab.

2. Lay tortillas out on a flat work surface. Spread one-fourth of the filling on half of each tortilla. Fold tortillas in half, pressing gently to flatten.

3. Heat 1 teaspoon olive oil in a large nonstick skillet over medium heat. Place two quesadillas in the pan and cook 3 to 4 minutes on each side until golden brown on both sides.

4. Transfer to a cutting board and tent with foil to keep warm. Repeat with the remaining 1 teaspoon oil and two quesadillas.

5. Cut each quesadilla into 4 wedges. Serve with a side salad or carrot sticks.

Nutritional Info: Calories: 290 | Sodium: 723 mg | Dietary Fiber 2.7 g | Total Fat: 16.1 g | Total Carbs: 22.8 g | Protein: 14.7 g.

Grilled Chicken and Fruit Tacos

Servings: 5 | Prep Time: 20 minutes | Cook Time: 25 minutes

Lighten up Taco Tuesday with these tasty fruit filled tacos with savory grilled chicken. Clean eating at its finest, these grilled chicken and fruit tacos are also paleo friendly and gluten free. Serve them with a side salad for extra antioxidant boosting super-food!

Ingredients:

2 plums, quartered and pitted

1 nectarine, quartered and pitted

1 medium red onion, diced

1 red jalapeno pepper, seeded and diced

2 tablespoons water

2 tablespoons olive oil

1 teaspoon sea salt

1 1/2 pounds boneless, skinless chicken thighs

1/2 teaspoon chipotle powder

1/2 teaspoon chili powder

1/2 teaspoon cumin powder

1/2 teaspoon dried oregano

1/4 cup cilantro, chopped

10 corn tortillas, made using Victoria Cast Iron tortilla press

1 cup romaine lettuce, shredded

Corn Tortillas:

1 cup masa harina

1 teaspoon sea salt

1 cup hot water

Sheet of plastic ziploc bag (cut in half)

[please see page 29 for instructions]

Instructions:

1. Pre-heat an oven to warm. Wrap tortillas in aluminum foil and place in oven.

2. Pre-heat a grill pan over medium-high heat. Add plums, nectarines, half of the chopped onions and half the chopped jalapeno, 1 tablespoon of the olive oil and 1/2 teaspoon salt to a mixing bowl and toss well.

3. Toss the chicken in a second mixing bowl with the chipotle powder, chili powder, cumin, oregano and remaining oil and salt.

4. Grill the fruit mix for 5 to 7 minutes, turning occasionally, until the fruit is slightly softened and charred. Transfer to a bowl.

5. Grill the chicken for 8 minutes on each side. Transfer to a cutting board. Use two forks and shred the chicken.

6. Place the rest of the jalapeno and onions in a food processor or blender with 2 tablespoons water. Blend until smooth.

7. Add about two-thirds of the grilled fruit to the processor or blender and pulse until slightly chunky. Transfer the salsa to a bowl and stir in the cilantro.

8. Remove the tortillas from the oven and evenly distribute the chicken down the middle of the tortillas. Top with fruit salsa and shredded lettuce. Fold and enjoy.

Nutritional Info: Calories: 1444 | Sodium: 578 mg | Dietary Fiber 6.6 g | Total Fat: 55.7 g | Total Carbs: 42.0 g | Protein: 185.6 g.

Grilled Chipotle Pork Tacos with Red Slaw

Servings: 4 | Prep Time: 10 minutes | Cook Time: 15 minutes

Grillmasters, unite! This recipe is right up your grilling alley. Perfectly marinated pork with tangy slaw has never been so easy. This recipe will surely turn one killer favorite in no time. You can even prep it all the day before the big barbecue and grill something special for friends and family.

Ingredients:

For the Red Slaw:

2 cups red cabbage, shredded

1/4 cup cilantro, finely chopped

1 tablespoon olive oil

1 tablespoon apple cider vinegar

1/4 teaspoon chipotle chili powder

1 small red pepper, thinly sliced

1/4 small red onion, thinly sliced

1/4 teaspoon sea salt

1/4 teaspoon coarse black pepper

1/4 teaspoon sugar substitute

For the Pork:

1/4 cup cilantro, finely chopped

1 tablespoon lime juice

1 tablespoon olive oil

1 teaspoon chipotle chili powder

2 cloves garlic, minced

1/4 cup red onion, very thinly sliced

1 (12-ounce) pork fillet, cut into 1/2-inch thick slices

1/4 teaspoon sea salt

1/4 teaspoon coarse black pepper

For the Tacos:

8 corn tortillas, made using
Victoria Cast Iron tortilla press

Sour cream, for garnish

Lime wedges, for garnish

Corn Tortillas:

2 cups masa harina

1/2 tablespoon sea salt

1 1/2 cups hot water

sheet of plastic ziploc bag (cut in half)

[please see page 29 for instructions]

Instructions:

1. Combine the coriander, lime juice, oil, chili powder, garlic and onions in a large, shallow dish with a lid. Add the pork slices, cover and shake to coat. Set aside to marinate. Alternatively, you can marinate in the refrigerator up to 24 hours for loads of flavor.

2. Preheat a grill on medium-high heat.

3. Add all slaw ingredients to a large mixing bowl. Toss until well-blended and set aside.

4. Remove the pork from the marinade and season the pork on both sides with salt and pepper. Grill, turning once, for 10 minutes: until browned and still slightly rosy inside. Transfer to a large plate.

5. Grill the tortillas for one minute on each side until grill marks appear and the tortillas are softened. Transfer to individual plates.

6. Divide the pork amongst the tortillas. Top with slaw. Serve with a spoonful of sour cream and a lime wedges.

Nutritional Info: Calories: 381 | Sodium: 302 mg | Dietary Fiber: 4.1 g | Total Fat: 19.4 g | Total Carbs: 25.3 g | Protein: 27.0 g.

Grilled Courgette Quesadilla

Servings: 4 | Prep Time: 10 minutes | Cook Time: 20 minutes

Go Mediterranean style when you grill up these tantalizing courgette quesadillas! Packed with healthy veggies and legumes, this quesadilla is sure to warm you up on a cool day. Serve with a side salad or fresh fruit to really kick up the clean eating a notch!

Ingredients:

1 onion, finely chopped

4 teaspoons olive oil

4 garlic cloves, minced

2 teaspoons ground cumin

1 tablespoon tomato purée

2 tablespoons water

1 (15-ounce) can pinto beans, drained and rinsed

3 courgettes, sliced on the diagonal

1/2 teaspoon sea salt

1/2 teaspoon coarse ground black pepper

2 cups cheddar, shredded

1 (4-ounce) green chilies, drained

2 tablespoons cilantro, chopped

8 flour tortillas, made using Victoria Cast Iron tortilla press

Flour Tortillas:

3 1/2 cups all-purpose flour

3 tablespoons vegetable shortening, chilled

1 teaspoon sea salt

2 teaspoons baking powder

1 1/2 cups water

[please see page 31 for instructions]

Instructions:

1. Heat a large frying pan on medium heat. Fry the onion in half the olive oil for about 5 mins or until soft. Add garlic and cumin. Reduce heat to low and cook 1 minute more. Stir in the tomato purée, pinto beans and water. Mash beans with a fork and heat through; stirring frequently.

2. Add courgette, salt, pepper and remaining oil to a mixing bowl. Toss to coat well.

3. Heat a griddle on medium. Cook courgette for 2 minutes on each side until tender and grill marked. Set aside.

4. Add the cheese, chili and cilantro to a mixing bowl; blend well.

5. Lay tortillas on a flat work surface. Spread the bean mix over half of the tortillas. Lay courgette slices on top. Top evenly with 2 tablespoons cheese mix. Fold tortilla in half and press gently to flatten. Repeat with the remaining tortillas.

6. Place two quesadillas on the hot griddle pan. Cook for 1-2 minutes on each side until cheese is melted.

7. Remove from heat. Tent with aluminum foil to keep warm. Cook remaining quesadillas and serve warm.

Nutritional Info: Calories: 665 | Sodium: 746 mg | Dietary Fiber 22.0 g | Total Fat: 11.9 g | Total Carbs: 100.1 g | Protein: 41.8 g.

Grilled Salmon Soft Tacos

Servings: 4 | Prep Time: 10 minutes | Cook Time: 10 minutes

Turn Taco Night into something a little south of the border. Grilled salmon is the perfect stuffing for those who love to clean eat or just want to pack their diet with antioxidant rich fish. Serve these up with tortilla chips and salsa for a little something different during the week.

Ingredients:

2 tablespoons olive oil

1 tablespoon ancho chili powder

1 tablespoon fresh lime juice

1/4 teaspoon sea salt

1/8 teaspoon fresh ground pepper

4 (4-ounce) salmon fillets, about 1-inch thick, skin on

8 flour tortillas, warmed, made using Victoria Cast Iron tortilla press

1 bag cabbage slaw

1 cup salsa

1 cup mexican crema

Flour Tortillas:

2 cups all-purpose flour

4 1/2 teaspoons vegetable shortening, chilled

1/2 teaspoon sea salt

1 teaspoon baking powder

2/3 cups water

Sheet of plastic ziploc bag (cut in half)

[please see page 31 for instructions]

Instructions:

1.   Preheat a grill to medium-high.

2. Combine oil, ancho chili powder, lime juice, salt and pepper in a small mixing bowl. Rub the spice mix liberally over salmon.

3. Grill the salmon for 8 minutes, skin-side down, until it is just cooked through.

4. Transfer fillets to a cutting board and cut each lengthwise into 2 pieces and remove the skin.

5. Lay two tortillas on each plate. Evenly divide the salmon, cabbage slaw, salsa in the middle of each tortilla. Drizzle with fresh crema.

Nutritional Info: Calories: 346 | Sodium: 601 mg | Dietary Fiber 5.2 g | Total Fat: 15.8 g | Total Carbs: 28.6 g | Protein: 26.2 g.

Ham, Apple & Cheese Quesadilla

Servings: 2 | Prep Time: 10 minutes | Cook Time: 20 minutes

When it comes to whipping something up savory and with a hint of sweet for lunchtime, try the Ham, Apple and Cheese Quesadilla. Tantalizingly tart and served with creamy apple butter for dipping, this quesadilla is food fusion at its finest! Serve with a fresh garden salad or cup of soup for on amazing, healthy lunch.

Ingredients:

4 flour tortillas, made using Victoria Cast Iron tortilla press

olive oil cooking spray

1 tablespoon Dijon mustard

1 cup oaxaca cheese, grated

1/2 pound virginia ham, shaved

1/8 teaspoon fresh ground black pepper

1 1/2 tablespoons no-sugar-added apple butter, plus 1/2 cup for dipping

1 small apple, cut into very thin slices

Flour Tortillas:

1 cup all-purpose flour

3 teaspoons vegetable shortening, chilled

1/4 teaspoon sea salt

1/2 teaspoon baking powder

1/2 cup water

Sheet of plastic ziploc bag (cut in half)

[please see page 31 for instructions]

Instructions:

1. Preheat the oven to 200 degrees Fahrenheit.

2. Spray 4 of the tortillas with cooking spray. Lay the oiled tortillas on a large cutting board oiled-side down. Brush with the mustard and sprinkle with about

half of the cheese. Sprinkle cheese with pepper. Top each evenly with a thin layer of shaved ham. Top ham with the remaining cheese. Top cheese with a few thinly sliced apple.

3. Brush the apple butter evenly on the remaining tortillas. Lay the tortillas apple butter side down, on the apples, and firmly press the tortillas together to make a quesadilla. Spray top with cooking spray.

4. Heat a large nonstick frying pan over medium heat. Lay a quesadilla in pan and cook 2 minutes or until golden crisp and the cheese starts to melt. Flip and cook 2 to 3 minutes more.

5. Transfer to a baking sheet and keep warm in the oven. Repeat with the remaining quesadillas.
Cut the quesadillas into four triangles and serve with extra apple butter for dipping.

Nutritional Info: Calories: 323 | Sodium: 796 mg | Dietary Fiber 4.5 g | Total Fat: 12.6 g | Total Carbs: 32.8 g | Protein: 19.7 g.

Mexican Layered Bean Casserole

Servings: 4 | Prep Time: 10 minutes | Cook Time: 20 minutes

For those nights when dinner just isn't your strong suit, prepare a quick and easy Mexican Layered Bean Casserole. This scrumptious casserole will also spice things up at any party or potluck, too.

Ingredients:

1 (16-ounce) can pinto beans, rinsed and drained

1 (16-ounce) can black beans, rinsed and drained

2 teaspoons hot sauce

1 cup fresh salsa

6 corn tortillas, halved, made using Victoria Cast Iron tortilla press

1 cup cheddar cheese, shredded

1 cup sour cream

1 tablespoon lime, zest

1/2 cup chopped tomatoes

1/2 cup black olives, sliced

1 tablespoon cilantro, chopped

Corn Tortillas:

2 cups masa harina

1/2 tablespoon sea salt

1 1/2 cup hot water

Sheet of plastic ziploc bag (cut in half)

[please see page 29 for instructions]

Instructions:

1. Preheat an oven to 375 degrees Fahrenheit.
2. Mix the pinto beans, black beans, salsa and hot sauce in a medium bowl.

3. Lay 4 of the tortilla halves onto the bottom of a 9-inch pie pan. Top with 1/3 of the bean mix. Top beans with 1/4 cup of cheese. Top cheese with 4 more tortilla halves, another layer of bean mix, and an additional 1/4 cup of cheese. Top with remaining tortillas.

4. Cover the pie pan with aluminum foil.

5. Cook casserole for 15 to 20 minutes; until cheese is melted.

6. While casserole is cooking mix sour cream and lime zest.

7. Remove casserole from oven. Uncover and let cool for five minutes to ten minutes.

8. Top casserole with lime sour cream. Sprinkle with the leftover cheese, cilantro, chopped tomatoes and olives. Slice and serve immediately.

Nutritional Info: Calories: 569 | Sodium: 421 mg | Dietary Fiber: 19.5 g | Total Fat: 13.7 g | Total Carbs: 83.4 g | Protein: 30.6 g.

Mexican Turkey Quesadilla

Servings: 4 | Prep Time: 25 minutes | Cook Time: 25 minutes

A delicious healthy alternative to red meat, turkey makes one tantalizing quesadilla. For those who love to lean protein load this is a great meal for you! Serve with a side of greek yogurt or carrot sticks for one sincerely healthy alternative to eating a traditional sandwich.

Ingredients:

1 tablespoon olive oil

1 small onion, chopped

2 teaspoons cilantro, chopped

1 yellow pepper, deseeded and diced

2 poblano peppers, chopped and seeded

2 tomatoes, chopped

1 (4-ounce) can green chilies

2 turkey breasts, shredded

1/4 teaspoon sea salt

1/4 teaspoon black pepper

2 cups mexican cheese, shredded

8 flour tortillas, made using Victoria Cast Iron tortilla press

1/2 cup unsalted butter, melted for brushing

1/4 cup sour cream

1 cup guacamole

1 cup salsa

Lime wedges, for garnish

Flour Tortillas:

2 cups all-purpose flour

4 1/2 teaspoons vegetable shortening, chilled

1/2 teaspoon sea salt

1 teaspoon baking powder

2/3 cups water

Sheet of plastic ziploc bag (cut in half)

[please see page 31 for instructions]

193

Instructions:

1. Pre-heat oven to warm.

2. Heat olive oil in a frying pan on medium heat. Add onion and peppers. Cook 5 minutes until softened. Add cilantro, tomatoes, and chilies. Heat through for one minute.

3. Remove from heat and fold in shredded turkey breast, salt, pepper and cheese.

4. Lay 4 tortillas on a flat work space. Brush one side with butter; flip. Divide the turkey mixture evenly between the tortillas. Top with a tortilla buttered side up, and press down lightly.

5. Heat a second frying pan on medium-high heat. Carefully transfer one quesadilla to the frying pan and cook for 3 to 4 minutes on each side; or until golden crisp and cheese is melted.

6. Remove from the pan and set aside in oven to keep warm.
    Repeat the process with the remaining quesadillas.

7. Cut the quesadillas into quarters and serve with salsa, guacamole and a lime wedge.

Nutritional Info: Calories: 841 | Sodium: 1847 mg | Dietary 15.5 g | Total Fat: 56.5 g | Total Carbs: 62.3 g | Protein: 34.6 g.

Mexican-Style Chicken-Filled Tortillas

Servings: 4 | Prep Time: 5 minutes | Cook Time: 12 minutes

Go all out Mexican style when you stuff your Victoria Cast Iron pressed tortillas with savory, warm chicken! Serve with a side of Mexican rice and refried beans for an authentic Mexican restaurant style meal at home.

Ingredients:

Cooking spray

4 boneless skinless chicken breasts, cut into thin bite-size strips

1 cup frozen corn, thawed

1 cup salsa

1 (2-ounce) can sliced olives, drained

8 flour tortillas, made using Victoria Cast Iron tortilla press

Sour cream, for garnish

Salsa, for garnish

Flour Tortillas:

2 cups all-purpose flour

4 1/2 teaspoons vegetable shortening, chilled

1/2 teaspoon sea salt

1 teaspoon baking powder

2/3 cups water

Sheet of plastic ziploc bag (cut in half)

[please see page 31 for instructions]

Instructions:

1. Spray large nonstick skillet with cooking spray. Heat over medium-high heat until hot.

2. Add chicken; cook and stir 5 to 6 minutes or until no longer pink in center. Stir in corn, salsa and olives. Reduce heat to medium. Cook 4 to 6 minutes more.

3.   Warm tortillas in a microwave. Spoon 1/4 of chicken mixture onto half of each tortilla. Fold tortillas over.

4.   Serve with a side of sour cream salsa.

Nutritional Info: Calories: 447 | Sodium: 661 mg | Dietary Fiber 5.4 g | Total Fat: 14.1 g | Total Carbs: 33.8 g | Protein: 47.1 g.

Prawn Fajitas

Servings: 2-3 | Prep Time: 10 minutes | Cook Time: 15 minutes

Fresh seafood stuffed fajitas are a great way to try out fresh tortillas made with your Victoria Cast Iron Tortilla Press. Garnished with cool, creamy avocado drizzle and lime wedges—these fajitas are simply out of this world. Try serving with mango margaritas or limeade for a fun twist.

Ingredients:

2 limes, juiced, plus wedges for garnish

1 teaspoon lime zest

1 red jalapeno, seeded and chopped

2 garlic cloves, minced

1/4 cup cilantro, chopped

1/4 cup sour cream

8 ounces large prawn, raw and peeled

1 avocado, stoned, skinned and sliced

1 tablespoon olive oil

1 red pepper, seeded and sliced

5 corn tortillas, made using Victoria Cast Iron tortilla press

Corn Tortillas:

1/2 cup masa harina

1/2 teaspoon sea salt

1/2 cup hot water

Sheet of plastic ziploc bag (cut in half)

[please see page 29 for instructions]

Instructions:

1. Mix half the lime juice, half the jalapeno, half the garlic and half the cilantro in a mixing bowl. Add the prawns and toss well to coat. Set aside to marinate.

2. Add the avocado remaining lime juice, chili, garlic, 1/4 cup sour cream to a food processor. Process until smooth. Transfer to a serving bowl. Fold in the remaining cilantro and lime zest. Set aside.

3. Heat the olive oil in a frying pan. Cook the red pepper for 3 minutes, until it begins to soften. Add the prawns and fry, in a single layer, for 1-2 minutes on each side. When prawns turn pink and are firm to touch, transfer to a serving dish.

4. Serve prawn fajitas with warm tortillas, avocado cream and lime wedges.

Nutritional Info: Calories: 607 | Sodium: 325 mg | Dietary Fiber 12.8 g | Total Fat: 36.3 g | Total Carbs: 43.5 g | Protein: 32.7 g.

Pulled Pork Torta

Servings: 6 | Prep Time: 15 minutes | Cook Time: 40 minutes

Turn leftovers into something absolutely fabulous with this delicious Pulled Pork Torta. A one dish meal, this hot pot is so yummy the whole family will be asking for seconds. Simply use leftover pulled pork to turn your fresh Victoria Cast Iron pressed tortillas into one healthy main meal.

Ingredients:

3 cups pulled pork

1 (14-ounce) can no-added-salt diced tomatoes, drained and juice reserved

1/4 cup diced pepperoni

4 flour tortillas, made using Victoria Cast Iron tortilla press

3/4 cups shredded monterey jack cheese

1/4 cup finely chopped scallions for garnish

1/4 cup chopped fresh cilantro for garnish

Cooking spray

Flour Tortillas:

1 cup all-purpose flour

3 teaspoons vegetable shortening, chilled

1/4 teaspoon sea salt

1/2 teaspoon baking powder

1/2 cup water

Sheet of plastic ziploc bag (cut in half)

[please see page 31 for instructions]

Instructions:

1. Preheat oven to 375 degrees Fahrenheit. Coat a deep-dish pie pan with cooking spray.

2. Heat leftover pork and sauce in a sauce pot on medium heat just until warm. Fold in tomatoes and pepperoni. Mix well and remove from heat.

3. Spread about 1/2 cup of the pork mixture in the prepared pan to cover the bottom. Top with 1 tortilla. Spoon 1/3 of remaining mixture over the tortilla. Repeat twice, topping with the fourth tortilla. Drizzle the reserved tomato juice over the top and cover with foil.

4. Bake for 20 minutes. Remove the foil. Cover with cheese and continue baking 20 minutes more, uncovered, until the cheese is melted and the torta is bubbly.

5. Remove from oven and set aside to cool for 10 minutes.

6. Top with scallions and cilantro. Serve in individual bowls.

Nutritional Info: Calories: 247 | Sodium: 213 mg | Dietary Fiber 0.8 g | Total Fat: 10.2 g | Total Carbs: 2.7 g | Protein: 34.7 g.

Punjabi Quesadillas

Servings: 4 | Prep Time: 5 minutes | Cook Time: 30 minutes

Bring a taste of the far East right into the comfort of your own kitchen. If you love warm Indian food, you will love these Punjabi Quesadillas. Serve with a side of mango chutney for dipping and fall in love with super health boosting spices!

Ingredients:

2 tablespoons olive oil, plus more for brushing

1 teaspoon ginger, chopped

1/2 teaspoon garlic, minced

1 onion, finely chopped

1 teaspoon garam masala

1 teaspoon paprika

1 teaspoon cumin powder

1/2 teaspoon turmeric

1/8 teaspoon salt

1/8 teaspoon pepper

2 tablespoons tomato puree

2 chicken breasts, boneless and skinless, cut into 1 inch pieces

1/2 cup yogurt, plain

4 flour tortillas, made using Victoria Cast Iron tortilla press

1 cup mozzarella cheese, shredded

Flour Tortillas:

1 cup all-purpose flour

3 teaspoons vegetable shortening, chilled

1/4 teaspoon sea salt

1/2 teaspoon baking powder

1/2 cup water

Sheet of plastic ziploc bag (cut in half)

[please see page 31 for instructions]

Instructions:

1. Pour olive oil into a large frying pan. Heat on medium-high heat. Add the ginger, garlic and onion. Sauté for 3 minutes until golden soft. Add the spices and stir for 30 seconds; until fragrant. Reduce heat to low. Add the tomato puree, stirring well to incorporate.

2. Add the chicken pieces, stir well to coat and cook for about 5 to 6 minutes, until the chicken is almost cooked through. Fold in the yogurt and continue to cook until the chicken is done, about 3 to 4 minutes.

3. Preheat the oven to 400 degrees Fahrenheit. Lay tortillas on a baking sheet and brush with oil. Flip it and place oil side down on the baking sheet.

4. Cover with mozzarella. Add 1/3 of the chicken filling and spread it over the cheese. Top with more cheese. Cover with a second tortilla and brush the top with olive oil. Repeat with the remaining tortillas to build second quesadilla

5. Bake for 3 to 5 minutes, until the cheese is melted and the tortilla is slightly golden. Cut into wedges and serve.

Nutritional Info: Calories: 374 | Sodium: 465 mg | Dietary Fiber 2.7 g | Total Fat: 18.8 g | Total Carbs: 18.4 g | Protein: 32.9 g.

Quick Pulled Pork Tostadas

Servings: 8 | Prep Time: 20 minutes | Cook Time: 35 minutes

Yummy pulled pork topped tostadas are just the thing for a quick mid-week dinner. Cook the pork and tostadas in advance and store them in individual portions for family members to reheat when you need something super quick and easy. Filling and scrumptious, these tostadas really hit the healthy spot!

Ingredients:

1 tablespoon olive oil

1 small onion, finely chopped

2 cloves garlic, finely chopped

2 cups pico de gallo

1 (7-ounce) can chipotle peppers in adobo sauce

1/4 cup chicken broth

1 pork fillet, cut into 4 pieces

1 teaspoon cumin

1 teaspoon chili powder

1/4 teaspoon sea salt

1/2 teaspoon coarse ground black pepper

8 corn tortillas, warmed; made using Victoria Cast Iron tortilla press

1 cup romaine lettuce, shredded

1/2 cup monterey jack cheese, shredded

1/2 cup sour cream

Lime wedges, for garnish

Corn Tortillas:

1 cup masa harina

1 teaspoon sea salt

1 cup hot water

Sheet of plastic ziploc bag (cut in half)

[please see page 29 for instructions]

Instructions:

1. Puree the entire can of chipotle pepper with adobo sauce a food processor or blender.

2. Heat the olive oil in a frying pan over medium heat. Add the onions and cook, for 4 minutes, until the onions begin to soften. Add the garlic and cook for one minute.

3. Add 1/4 cup of pico de gallo and the chipotle adobo puree to the frying pan. Stir frequently, cook for 5 minutes, until the tomatoes begin to soften. Fold in the chicken broth and bring to a simmer.

4. Coat the pork pieces with cumin, chili powder, sea salt and pepper. Add pork to the frying pan and continue to simmer. Flip the pork and cover the frying pan. Reduce heat and cook until the pork is cooked through and tender, about 20 minutes.

5. Move an oven rack to the top, six inches away from the heat source. Pre-heat oven on high broil. Baste corn tortillas with olive oil on both sides. Place on an aluminum foil lined baking sheet. Broil two minutes and flip the tortillas. Cook 2 more minutes, until golden brown and crisp.

6. Transfer pork to a plate and cover with aluminum foil. Set aside to rest for 5 minutes.

7. Bring the sauce in the frying pan back to a good simmer. Turn down to medium-low heat and cook until thickened.

8. Shred the pork using two forks. Fold shredded pork into the sauce and toss well to coat. Cook for 5 minutes.

9. Divide the shredded pork evenly among the tostadas. Top with lettuce, cheese and the remaining pico de gallo. Drizzle with sour cream and serve with a lime wedge.

Nutritional Info: Calories: 232 | Sodium: 862.5 mg | Dietary Fiber: 3.8 g | Total Fat: 12.3 g | Total Carbs: 16 g | Protein: 12.9 g.

Shredded Beef Wet Burritos

Servings: 8 | Prep Time: 20 minutes | Cook Time: 4-6 hours, plus 15 minutes

Wet burritos make for some seriously wild comfort food. While this recipe takes a little longer than the others, the wait is so very worth it with these scrumptious Shredded Beef Wet Burritos. Try them on a fall weekend when you can have friends and family join in on the fun!

Ingredients:

For Shredded Beef:

1 (4-pound) beef rump roast

2 cups beef broth

For Burritos:

1 jar enchilada sauce

1 package taco seasoning

1 lime juiced

8 flour tortillas, made using Victoria Cast Iron tortilla press

2 cups cheddar cheese, shredded

1 cup iceberg lettuce, shredded for garnish

Sour cream, for garnish

Pickled jalapenos, for garnish

Flour Tortillas:

2 cups all-purpose flour

4 1/2 teaspoons vegetable shortening, chilled

Sheet of plastic ziploc bag (cut in half)

[please see page 31 for instructions]

1/2 teaspoon sea salt

1 teaspoon baking powder

2/3 cups water

Instructions:

1. Cut the rump roast into 3 inch chunks. Place the beef into the bottom of a slow cooker. Pour the beef broth over the meat, place the lid on the slow cooker, and cook on high for 4-6 hours; or until meat is tender.

2. Pull the chunks of beef out of the cooking liquid and shred it with two forks on a cutting board. Set aside.

3. Combine enchilada sauce and taco seasoning in a mixing bowl.

4. Preheat oven to 350 degrees.

5. Lay tortillas on a flat work surface. Stuff evenly with beef and the cheese. Roll them up and lay tightly in a large baking dish. Top with sauce.

6. Bake for 15 minutes.

7. Plate and top with lettuce, sour cream and jalapenos.

Nutritional Info: Calories: 607 | Sodium: 531 mg | Dietary Fiber 2.3 g | Total Fat: 24.7 g | Total Carbs: 13.7 g | Protein: 78.8 g.

Shrimp and Avocado Sushi Rolls

Servings: 6 | Prep Time: 10-15 minutes | Cook Time: 10 minute

Get crafty when making meals with your Victoria Cast Iron Tortilla press and whip up some delicious Shrimp and Avocado Sushi Rolls. These delicious creamy filled rolls are fresh and filled with lean protein and super-antioxidant boosting veggies. Serve them up in slices for a party or keep them rolled for individual mealtime fun!

Ingredients

2 cups short-grain sushi rice, cooked and cooled

1 teaspoon wasabi powder

1 teaspoon water

2 teaspoons soy sauce

2 tablespoons chopped green onions

1 teaspoon mayonnaise

1/8 teaspoon hot pepper flakes

8 flour tortillas, made using Victoria Cast Iron tortilla press

6 sheets nori

1 1/2 pounds shrimp, cooked, peeled and chopped

1 cup avocado chopped

1 cup cucumber, finely chopped

1/3 cup soy sauce

Black sesame seeds, for garnish

1/2 cup pickled ginger for serving

Flour Tortillas:

2 cups all-purpose flour

4 1/2 teaspoons vegetable shortening, chilled

1/2 teaspoon sea salt

1 teaspoon baking powder

2/3 cups water

Sheet of plastic ziploc bag (cut in half)

[please see page 31 for instructions

207

Instructions

1. Combine wasabi and water in mixing bowl. Add 2 tablespoons soy sauce and mix well.

2. In a medium bowl, combine rice, wasabi mix, green onions, mayonnaise and hot pepper flakes.

3. Line each tortilla with sheets of nori. Distribute rice mixture equally in the center of each wrap. Top with shrimp, avocado and cucumber.

4. Fold both ends of the tortilla over the filling. Roll up and top with black sesame seeds. Serve with soy sauce and pickled ginger on the side.

Nutritional Info: Calories: 765 | Sodium: 1821 mg | Dietary 8.8 g | Total Fat: 12.7 g | Total Carbs: 108.9 g | Protein: 52.3 g.

Smoked Salmon Rotollos

Servings: 25 | Prep Time: 10 minutes | Cook Time: 10 minutes

Whip up some super-classy canapes for your next party using your Victoria Cast Iron Tortilla Press. Smoked Salmon Rotollos are so fancy, your friends will want to know who your caterer is!

Ingredients:

2 (8-ounce) packages cream cheese, room temperature

1 tablespoon lemon juice

2 tablespoons dill, chopped

1/2 teaspoon fresh ground black pepper

8 flour tortillas, made using Victoria Cast Iron tortilla press

12 ounces smoked salmon

Flour Tortillas:

2 cups all-purpose flour

4 1/2 teaspoons vegetable shortening, chilled

1/2 teaspoon sea salt

1 teaspoon baking powder

2/3 cups water

Sheet of plastic ziploc bag (cut in half)

[please see page 31 for instructions]

Instructions:

1. Whip the cream cheese with the lemon juice, chopped dill and black pepper.
2. Spread evenly across the flour tortillas. Cover cream cheese with the smoked salmon. Roll up like a burrito. Trim off the ends and discard.
3. Wrap rolls tightly in plastic wrap, twisting the ends firmly to enclose.
4. Slice on the diagonal. Unwrap and serve.

Nutritional Info: Calories: 88 | Sodium: 328 mg | Dietary Fiber 0 g | Total Fat: 7.0 g | Total Carbs: 2.4 g | Protein: 4.1 g.

Steak and Black Bean Chalupas

Servings: 5-7 | Prep Time: 15 minutes | Cook Time: 20 minutes

Whip up some delicious, nutritious and super flavorful Steak and Black Bean Chalupas for lunch or dinner with this tantalizing recipe. Creamy black beans and juicy steak piled on fried tortillas are so very filling, too. Chalupas really are the perfect treat for days when you sincerely crave comfort food with a spicy kick!

Ingredients:

2/3 cups beef broth

1/4 cup tequila (optional)

2 tablespoons fresh lime juice

1 pound steak, sliced in 1/4-inch-thick strips

For Corn Tortillas:

1 cup masa harina

1 teaspoon sea salt

1 cup hot water

Sheet of plastic ziploc bag (cut in half)

[please see page 29 for instructions]

For Black Beans:

1 (15-ounce) can black beans, rinsed and drained

2 teaspoons olive oil

1 cup onion, chopped

1 teaspoon chili powder

1 teaspoon cumin

1 teaspoon hot sauce

1/2 teaspoon sea salt

211

For Frying Steak:

4 tablespoons olive oil

1 teaspoon garlic powder

1 teaspoon chili powder

1/2 teaspoon dried oregano

1/4 teaspoon sea salt

1/2 teaspoon finely grated lime zest

10 corn tortillas, made using the Victoria Cast Iron tortilla press

Lime wedges, for serving

Sour cream, for serving

2 tablespoons pickled jalapenos, for garnish

Instructions

1. Marinate the steak in 1/3 cup beef broth, 2 tablespoons fresh lime juice, and 1/4 cup of tequila for two to 24 hours; covered in the refrigerator.

2. Drain the steak and let the meat come to room temperature.

3. Prepare the beans to by heating 2 teaspoons of olive oil in a medium saucepan over medium heat. Add the chopped onions and sauté for five minutes. Stir in chili powder and cumin and cook for 15 seconds until fragrant. Add the black beans, hot sauce and sea salt. Fold in 1/3 cup beef broth. Stir well. Bring to a boil. Cover and turn heat to low. Simmer for 15 minutes.

4. Prepare the tortillas by preheating the oven to 350 degrees Fahrenheit. Lay the tortillas on a baking sheet, brush both sides with the oil and sprinkle with salt. Bake until golden brown and crispy, about 10 minutes.

5. Use a potato masher and smash the black beans well. Stir to mix in the broth and make a thick bean mixture. Cook for five additional minutes, then remove from the heat; keep covered.

6. Remove tortillas from the oven and set aside to cool.

7. Heat 2 tablespoons of olive oil in a large skillet over high heat until lightly smoking.

8.   Mix the remaining sea salt and chili powder with the garlic powder and oregano in a small bowl. Toss the steak strips in the seasoning mix; coat well.

9.   Add the seasoned steak strips to the frying pan. Stir in lime zest. Toss continually for 1 to 2 minutes until the strips are browned on both sides. Transfer steak to a paper towel lined plate to remove excess grease.

10. Assemble the chalupas by spreading a thin layer of smashed black beans on each crispy corn tortilla. Divide the steak among the chalupas. Top with jalapenos and sour cream. Serve with a lime wedge on the side.

Nutritional Info: Calories: 512, Sodium: 602 mg, Dietary Fiber: 11.6 g, Total Fat: 14.4 g, Total Carbs: 53.2 g, Protein: 38.9 g.

Steak Burritos

Servings: 4 | Prep Time: 30 minutes | Cook Time: 30 minutes

If you're craving Baja style burritos packed full of meat, beans, rice, cheese, guacamole and salsa, then these scrumptious Steak Burritos are going to really hit the spot. Served with a side of chipotle salsa, chips and an ice cold beer—this recipe makes for one seriously rad meal!

Ingredients:

1/2 cup salsa

1/2 cup water

1/4 cup instant brown rice

1 (15-ounce) can black beans, drained and rinsed

12 ounce strip steak, trimmed and thinly sliced crosswise

1/4 teaspoon sea salt

1/4 teaspoon freshly ground pepper

1/2 teaspoon garlic powder

1 tablespoon olive oil

4 flour tortillas, made using Victoria Cast Iron tortilla press

1/2 cup sharp cheddar cheese, shredded

1/4 cup prepared guacamole

2 tablespoons cilantro, chopped

Flour Tortillas:

1 cup all-purpose flour

3 teaspoons vegetable shortening, chilled

1/4 teaspoon sea salt

1/2 teaspoon baking powder

1/2 cup water

Sheet of plastic ziploc bag (cut in half)

[please see page 31 for instructions]

Instructions:

1. Combine salsa and water in a small saucepan; bring to a boil. Stir in rice, reduce heat to a simmer, cover and cook for 5 minutes.

2. Add beans to rice and return to a simmer. Cook 5 minutes more, uncovered, stirring occasionally, until the rice is tender and most of the liquid is absorbed.

3. Season steak with salt, pepper and garlic powder.

4. Heat olive oil in a large frying over medium-high heat. Add steak and cook 3-5 minutes, stirring occasionally, until browned and cooked through.

5. Lay tortillas on a flat work surface. Divide the steak among the tortillas evenly. Top with equal amounts of cheese, guacamole, cilantro and the rice mixture down the middle. Roll each tortilla up into a burrito and serve.

Nutritional Info: Calories: 756 | Sodium: 521 mg | Dietary Fiber 19.4 g | Total Fat: 18.0 g | Total Carbs: 90.1 g | Protein: 60.4 g.

Tex Wassabi's Koi Fish Tacos

Servings: 5 | Prep Time: 20 minutes | Cook Time: 15 minutes

One of the most delicious ways to enjoy a fresh pressed tortilla is stuffed with battered fish, topped with pico de gallo and tequila lime aioli. This delicious recipe brightens up any mild white fish, and is best served with an ice cold cerveza on the side.

Ingredients:

Battered Fish:

1 lime, juiced

15 ml white tequila

1 teaspoon sea salt

1 teaspoon black pepper

1/2-pound cod, cut into 1-inch pieces

1 cup flour

1 1/2 cup beer

2 eggs

1/4 teaspoon sea salt

1/4 teaspoon coarse ground pepper

Olive oil, for frying

10 corn tortillas, made using Victoria Cast Iron tortilla press

Tequila Lime Aioli:

3 tablespoons white tequila, like Espolon

2 tablespoons lime juice

1/4 teaspoon lime zest

1/2 cup sour cream

1/4 teaspoon

1 teaspoon minced garlic

1/4 teaspoon sea salt

Corn Tortillas:

2 cups masa harina

1/2 tablespoon sea salt

1 1/2 cups hot water

Sheet of plastic ziploc bag (cut in half)

[please see page 29 for instructions]

Tacos:

1/4 cup white cabbage, shredded

1/4 cup red cabbage, shredded

3 tablespoons cilantro, chopped

1 cup pico de gallo

1 lime, sliced into wedges

Instructions

1. Combine the juice of one lime, 15 ml white tequila, sea salt and pepper in a mixing bowl. Add the fish and toss to coat. Set aside to marinate for 15 minutes.
2. Prepare the Tequila Lime Aioli by whisking all of the ingredients together in a large mixing bowl. Cover with plastic wrap and set in the refrigerator so flavors marinate well.
3. Preheat oven to 350 degrees Fahrenheit.
4. Combine flour, eggs and beer in a shallow mixing bowl, and lightly whisk as to not froth the beer.
5. Remove the fish from the marinade and dredge in the beer batter.
6. Heat the olive oil in a frying pan on medium-high heat. Fry the fish in a single layer, about 5 minutes on each side, until golden brown.
7. Wrap tortillas in foil and place in the preheated oven. Turn temperature to warm while fish is frying.
8. Place fish on a paper towel lined plate to soak up excess grease.
9. Remove the tortillas and place one or two per plate.
10. Distribute the fish evenly amongst the tortillas. Top evenly with cabbage, cilantro, pico de gallo, and tequila lime aioli. Serve with a lime wedge.

Nutritional Info: Calories: 293 | Sodium: 614 mg | Dietary Fiber: 4.2 g | Total Fat: 5.9 g | Total Carbs: 39.6 g | Protein: 13.1 g.

Tortilla Crusted Catfish Po'Boys

Servings: 4 | Prep Time: 10 minutes | Cook Time: 15 minutes

Southern fusion is one tastefully popular way to use your Victoria Cast Iron Tortilla Press when you whip up some fresh tortillas. Whether you're a Southern foodie expert or just want to try something new—Tortilla Crusted Catfish Po' Boys will surely hit the southern fried spot!

Ingredients:

2 (8-ounce) catfish fillets

5 corn tortillas, cut into strips; made using Victoria Cast Iron tortilla press

1/4 cup parmesan cheese, grated

3 tablespoons Cajun seasoning, like Chef Paul Prudhomme's Meat Magic seasoning

1/2 teaspoon kosher salt

1/2 teaspoon finely ground black pepper

1 cup buttermilk

4 cups rapeseed oil

1/2 cup sugar-free mayonnaise

4 hoagie rolls, toasted

2 cups iceberg lettuce, shredded

1 large tomato, sliced

Hot sauce, like Tabasco

Corn Tortillas:

1/2 cup masa harina

1/2 teaspoon sea salt

1/2 cup hot water

Sheet of plastic ziploc bag (cut in half)

[please see page 29 for instructions]

Instructions:

1. Cut the catfish into 2-inch strips. Pat dry and set aside.

2. Add the tortillas to a food processor and pulse until finely ground and transfer to a shallow mixing bowl.

3. Stir together Parmesan, salt, pepper and 1 tablespoon of the Cajun seasoning in a separate mixing bowl.

4. Shake the buttermilk for one minute. Pour into another separate metal mixing bowl and whisk 1 tablespoon of the Cajun seasoning into the buttermilk.

5. Add the rapeseed oil to large, heavy-bottomed pot and bring to 350 degrees Fahrenheit over medium-high heat.

6. Toss the catfish with the seasoned Parmesan.

7. Divide the catfish strips into two batches. Dip the first batch in the buttermilk; shake excess off. Then dredge each piece in the ground tortillas.

8. Gently transfer to the oil and fry 5 minutes or until golden. Transfer cooked catfish to a paper towel lined plate. Repeat with the second batch.

9. Whisk the mayonnaise and the remaining tablespoon Cajun seasoning together in a small bowl. Spread evenly on the toasted rolls.

10. Top one side with iceberg and tomato slices and the other with an even layer of catfish. Serve with hot sauce.

Nutritional Info: Calories: 649 | Sodium: 1057 mg | Dietary 10.1 g | Total Fat: 26.2 g | Total Carbs: 73.3 g | Protein: 37.2 g.

Turkey Club Tortilla Pinwheels

Servings: 12 | Prep Time: 20 minutes | Cook Time: 10 minute

Get your party platter on with these delicious, easy Turkey Club Tortillas Pinwheels. Cool and spicy, these pinwheels will surely become a party or family gathering favorite.

Ingredients:

Turkey Club Pinwheel:

4 flour tortillas, made using Victoria Cast Iron tortilla press

1 pound deli turkey, shaved

1 cup tomatoes, thinly sliced

1 package mexican cheese, shredded

1 cup bacon, cooked until crisp and crumbled

Romaine lettuce, washed and sliced

Flour Tortillas:

1 cup all-purpose flour

3 teaspoons vegetable shortening, chilled

1/4 teaspoon sea salt

1/2 teaspoon baking powder

1/2 cup water

Sheet of plastic ziploc bag (cut in half)

[please see page 31 for instructions]

Spicy Mayo:

1/4 cup sugar-free mayonnaise

1/4 teaspoon salt

1/4 teaspoon garlic powder

1/8 teaspoon onion powder

1/8 teaspoon paprika

1/8 teaspoon chili powder

1/8 teaspoon cayenne pepper

Instructions:

1. Combine all spicy mayo dip ingredients together in a mixing bowl. Set aside until ready to use.

2. Lay tortillas on a flat surface. Spread spicy mayo over half the tortilla. Sprinkle cheese over mayo. Top with turkey and tomatoes. Sprinkle with bacon, and top with lettuce.

3. Roll very tightly around the stuffing. Secure with plastic wrap. Repeat with remaining ingredients until all tortillas are rolled.

4. Slice tortilla in 2-inch-thick pinwheels while still in plastic wrap. Unwrap and stack pinwheels on a serving tray. Serve immediately, or keep in the refrigerator for up to one day.

Nutritional Info: Calories: 193 | Sodium: 946 mg | Dietary Fiber 0.9 g | Total Fat: 11.7 g | Total Carbs: 8.8 g | Protein: 13.3 g.

11

Tortilla Desserts

Apple/Peach Turnovers

Servings: 8 | Prep Time: 10 minutes | Cook Time: 30 minutes

Turn your Victoria Cast Iron tortilla press into a dessert making dream. Quick and easy apple/peach turnovers are an absolute delight. Try serving them with vanilla ice cream right out of the oven for a truly decadent dessert.

Ingredients:

8 flour tortillas, made using Victoria Cast Iron tortilla press

1 (20-ounce) can apple or peach pie filling

2 sticks unsalted butter

1 cup sugar

1 teaspoon cinnamon

Cooking spray

Flour Tortillas:

2 cups all-purpose flour

4 1/2 teaspoons vegetable shortening, chilled

1/2 teaspoon sea salt

1 teaspoon baking powder

2/3 cups water

Sheet of plastic ziploc bag (cut in half)

[please see page 31 for instructions]

Instructions:

1. Pre-heat oven to 350 degrees Fahrenheit.
2. Fill each of the tortillas with 1 tablespoon of pie filling and fold in half.
3. Spray a 9x11-inch baking pan with cooking spray.
4. Place filled tortillas in pan.

5.   Add butter, sugar, spices and water to a saucepan and bring to a boil on medium-high heat. Stir constantly, gently, until sugar is dissolved and butter melts. Pour over rolled tortillas.

6.   Bake on middle rack for 30 minutes or until golden brown.

Nutritional Info: Calories: 386 | Sodium: 174 mg | Dietary Fiber 3.4 g | Total Fat: 23.7 g | Total Carbs: 45.7 g | Protein: 1.8 g.

Baked Cinnamon Sugar Tortilla Bowls

Servings: 4 | Prep Time: 5 minutes | Cook Time: 18 minutes

Bake up some super sweet Cinnamon Sugar Tortilla Bowls for dessert. The stuffing possibilities are endless with these tantalizing treats. Think ice cream, fried ice cream, yogurt, granola and pouring yogurt, cream cheese and fruit—anything your sweet little heart desires.

Ingredients:

4 flour tortillas, made using Victoria Cast Iron tortilla press

1/4 cup unsalted butter, melted for brushing

5 tablespoons sugar

1 tablespoon cinnamon

Flour Tortillas:

1 cup all-purpose flour

3 teaspoons vegetable shortening, chilled

1/4 teaspoon sea salt

1/2 teaspoon baking powder

1/2 cup water

Sheet of plastic ziploc bag (cut in half)

[please see page 31 for instructions]

Instructions:

1. Pre-heat oven to 350 degrees Fahrenheit.
2. Lightly brush both sides of each tortilla with melted butter and generously sprinkle with cinnamon sugar.
3. Gently press each tortilla into an oven safe bowl; fold where needed.

4. Place bowls in preheated oven on middle rack and bake for 15 minutes or until they golden crisp.

5. Remove from oven and set aside for 2-3 minutes. Remove them from their bowls. Place the tortilla bowls on wax paper to finish cooling.

6. Fill with your favorite treats and enjoy!

Nutritional Info: Calories: 215 | Sodium: 93 mg | Dietary Fiber 2.4 g | Total Fat: 12.2 g | Total Carbs: 27.1 g | Protein: 1.6 g.

Banana-Caramel Tortilla Tarts

Servings: 4 | Prep Time: 5 minutes | Cook Time: 25 minutes

Delectably delicious, these Banana-Caramel Tortilla Tarts are just the thing for any lover of creamy caramel topped easy desserts. Serve it up with a side of greek vanilla yogurt and a hint of cinnamon for a super dreamy tortilla treat.

Ingredients:

4 flour tortillas, made using Victoria Cast Iron tortilla press

2 tablespoons unsalted butter, melted

1 teaspoon olive oil

5 tablespoons sugar or sugar substitute

6 bananas, peeled and sliced

1 tablespoon lemon juice

Caramel sauce, for topping

Flour Tortillas:

1 cup all-purpose flour

3 teaspoons vegetable shortening, chilled

1/4 teaspoon sea salt

1/2 teaspoon baking powder

1/2 cup water

Sheet of plastic ziploc bag (cut in half)

[please see page 31 for instructions]

Instructions:

1. Pre-heat an oven to 425 degrees Fahrenheit.
2. Line two baking sheets with aluminum foil and set aside.
3. Combine butter and olive oil in small mixing bowl.
4. Brush each tortilla on both sides with the butter and sprinkle all tortillas with 1 tablespoon of sugar. Lay them in a single layer on the lined baking sheets.

228

5.   Toss the bananas with the lemon juice in a mixing bowl. Divide evenly, and top the tortillas with the bananas. Sprinkle with the remaining sugar.

6.   Bake the tortillas for 11 to 13 minutes, switching the sheets halfway through, until golden crisp. Drizzle with the caramel sauce and serve!

Nutritional Info: Calories: 328 | Sodium: 54 mg | Dietary Fiber: 6.1 g | Total Fat: 8.2 g | Total Carbs: 66.2 g | Protein: 3.4 g.

Cinnamon and Sugar Tortilla Strips

Servings: 6-8 | Prep Time: 5 minutes | Cook Time: 6 minutes

Sweeten things up with some super tasty tortilla strips! Great to snack on. These sugary sweet tortilla strips are also delicious on Greek yogurt or ice cream. Try it on top of your morning oatmeal to add a crunchy sweet treat to fuel the day. No matter which way you love to eat them, you'll also love how easy it is to make them!

Ingredients:

3 flour tortillas, made using Victoria Cast Iron tortilla press

4 tablespoons unsalted butter

3 tablespoons granulated sugar or sugar substitute

1/2 teaspoon ground cinnamon

Vanilla ice cream or Greek yogurt

Flour Tortillas:

1 cup all-purpose flour

3 teaspoons vegetable shortening, chilled

1/4 teaspoon sea salt

1/2 teaspoon baking powder

1/2 cup water

Sheet of plastic ziploc bag (cut in half)

[please see page 31 for instructions]

Instructions:

1. Cut the tortillas into 1/2-inch-thick strips.
2. Heat the butter and sugar in a large nonstick frying pan over medium-low heat.
3. Fold in the tortilla strips when butter is melted.
4. Cook for 5 minutes, stirring frequently, until the tortillas are golden brown and crisp.

5.   Transfer to a parchment lined baking sheet in a single layer. Sprinkle with cinnamon. Serve with vanilla ice cream or greek yogurt.

Nutritional Info: Calories: 117 | Sodium: 60 mg | Dietary Fiber 0.9 g | Total Fat: 8.0 g | Total Carbs: 11.5 g | Protein: 0.8 g.

Cinnamon Tortilla Sundaes

Servings: 4 | Prep Time: 5 minutes | Cook Time: 25 minutes

Take clean eating to a whole new level when you whip up one simply sweet treat with this delicious recipe for Cinnamon Tortilla Sundaes. The perfect snack on a warm sunny day, these sundaes are sure to become a favorite to make with fresh tortillas from your Victoria Cast Iron Tortilla Press!

Ingredients:

4 flour tortillas, cut into triangles; made using Victoria Cast Iron tortilla press

2 tablespoons unsalted butter, melted

2 teaspoons olive oil

2 tablespoons sugar or sugar substitute like Splenda

2 teaspoons cinnamon

No-added sugar vanilla ice cream

Fresh cherries, seeded and chopped

Almonds, chopped

Sugar-free hot fudge sauce

Flour Tortillas:

1 cup all-purpose flour

3 teaspoons vegetable shortening, chilled

1/4 teaspoon sea salt

1/2 teaspoon baking powder

1/2 cup water

Sheet of plastic ziploc bag (cut in half)

[please see page 31 for instructions]

Instructions:

1. Pre-heat an oven to 425 degrees Fahrenheit.

232

2.   Line a baking sheet with aluminum foil and set aside.

3.   Combine sugar and cinnamon in a small mixing bowl.

4.   Combine butter and olive oil in separate mixing bowl.

5.   Brush the tortilla triangles on both sides with the butter and sprinkle with the sugar and cinnamon mix. Lay them in a single layer on the lined baking sheet.

6.   Bake the tortillas, flipping once, 5 to 7 minutes per side; until golden crisp. Transfer to a plate and set aside to cool for five minutes.

7.   Equally distribute triangles into four individual bowls. Top cinnamon sugar tortillas with the ice cream, almonds, hot fudge sauce and cherries.

Nutritional Info: Calories: 149 | Sodium: 52 mg | Dietary Fiber: 2.1 g | Total Fat: 8.8 g | Total Carbs: 17.6 g | Protein: 1.5 g.

Dessert Nachos

Servings: 8 | Prep Time: 15 minutes | Cook Time: 12 minutes

Switch things up with a killer new take on yummy nachos—go dessert style! Dessert nachos one really sweet treat to serve up at any party or family movie night.

Ingredients:

4 teaspoons cinnamon

1 tablespoon sugar

8 flour tortillas, cut into triangles, made using Victoria Cast Iron tortilla press

6 tablespoons unsalted butter, melted

1 cup strawberries, chopped

1 banana, sliced

3 scoops vanilla ice cream

Hot fudge, for garnish

Whip cream, for garnish

Flour Tortillas:

2 cups all-purpose flour

4 1/2 teaspoons vegetable shortening, chilled

1/2 teaspoon sea salt

1 teaspoon baking powder

2/3 cups water

Sheet of plastic ziploc bag (cut in half)

[please see page 31 for instructions]

Instructions:

1. Preheat oven to 350 degrees Fahrenheit.
2. Combine tortilla triangles and melted butter in a large mixing bowl. Toss to coat.
3. Transfer chips to an aluminum foil lined baking sheet.
4. Dust with cinnamon sugar.

5. Bake 10-12 minutes or until puffed up and just turning golden crisp. Remove from oven and let cool.

6. Arrange cooled cinnamon chips on a plate. Top with ice cream, strawberries, banana, hot fudge and whip cream.

Nutritional Info: Calories: 179 | Sodium: 82 mg | Dietary Fiber 2.1 g | Total Fat: 10.7 g | Total Carbs: 20.6 g | Protein: 2.2 g.

Firehouse Frito Pie

Servings: 8 | Prep Time: 1 hour | Cook Time: 1 hour

Fire things up at dinner time with this fresh new take on the Frito Pie. This modern twist on the classic recipe is packed with one fresh, healthy punch. A light take on the classic, Firehouse Frito Pie is delicious garnished with cool, creamy sour cream and fresh shredded lettuce!

Ingredients:

1 tablespoon olive oil

1 large onion, chopped

1 pound 93%-lean ground turkey

1/2 cup mild chili powder

1 teaspoon ground cumin

1 large zucchini, peeled and shredded

1 (28-ounce) can diced tomatoes

1 cup reduced-sodium beef broth

16 corn tortillas, made using Victoria Cast Iron tortilla press

Cooking spray

2 (15-ounce) cans red kidney beans, drained and rinsed

2 cups sharp cheddar cheese, shredded

1 tomato, diced

2 cups iceberg lettuce, shredded

1 cup low-fat sour cream

Pickled jalapeños, for garnish

Corn Tortillas:

2 cups masa harina

1/2 tablespoon sea salt

1 1/2 cups hot water

Sheet of plastic ziploc bag (cut in half)

[please see page 29 for instructions]

Instructions:

1. Position racks in the middle and lower third of oven; preheat to 375 degrees Fahrenheit.

2. Heat oil in a Dutch oven over medium heat. Add onion and turkey. Cook for 5 minutes, breaking up with a spoon and stirring, until the turkey is no longer pink.

3. Add chili powder and cumin; cook, stirring, for 1 minute. Add zucchini, tomatoes and broth. Bring to a simmer. Partially cover and cook, stirring occasionally 30 minutes; maintaining a simmer.

4. Coat both sides of each tortilla with olive oil. Cut in half, then cut each half into 1-inch strips. Spread the strips evenly onto 2 large rimmed baking sheets. Bake, rotating the pans from top to bottom and stirring halfway through, until crisp, about 25 minutes.

5. Mash 1 cup kidney beans in a mixing bowl. After the chili has simmered for 30 minutes, stir in the mashed beans and whole beans. Cook until the beans are heated through, about 3 minutes more.

6. Place 3/4 cups tortilla strips in a shallow bowl. Ladle about 1 1/4 cups chili on top. Top chili with cheese, tomato, lettuce, scallions, pickled jalapeños and sour cream.

Nutritional Info: Calories: 939 | Sodium: 552 mg | Dietary Fiber 24.1 g | Total Fat: 37.0 g | Total Carbs: 100.6 g | Protein: 59.9 g.

Guacamole Ice Cream Cones

Servings: 8 | Prep Time: 10 minutes | Cook Time: 8 minutes

Looking for a more healthy way to enjoy guacamole? These Guacamole Ice Cream Cones are just the thing for all—you guacamole lovers at heart. Packed full of healthy fats and antioxidants, when paired with fresh tortillas—this really is the perfect way to snack clean and healthy.

Ingredients:

5 corn tortillas, made using Victoria Cast Iron tortilla press

1 ripe avocado, mashed

2 teaspoons lime juice

1/4 teaspoon sugar substitute

1/4 teaspoon sea salt

1/4 teaspoon coarse ground black pepper

1 teaspoon chili powder

1/2 cup olive oil, for brushing

1/4 cup tomatoes, chopped for garnish

Corn Tortillas:

1/2 cup masa harina

1/2 teaspoon sea salt

1/2 cup hot water

sheet of plastic ziploc bag (cut in half)

[please see page 29 for instructions]

Instructions

1. Pre-heat an oven to 350 degrees Fahrenheit.
2. Line a baking sheet with aluminum foil or parchment paper.
3. Lay the tortillas on a flat surface. Slice each tortilla in half.
4. Roll each tortilla into a cone shape and secure with a toothpick.

5. Brush each cone with olive oil and dust with chili powder.

6. Place the cones on the lined baking sheet and bake for 8 minutes.

7. While tortillas are baking add avocado to a mixing bowl and gently mash. Fold in lime juice, sugar substitute, sea salt and black pepper; blend well.

8. Remove tortillas from oven. Let cool for 3-5 minutes. Spoon guacamole into cones. Top each with chopped tomatoes and enjoy!

Nutritional Info: Calories: 242 | Sodium: 90 mg | Dietary Fiber: 3.3 g | Total Fat: 23.8 g | Total Carbs: 9.1 g | Protein: 1.5 g.

Tortilla and Black Bean Pie

Servings: 4 | Prep Time: 10 minutes | Cook Time: 15 minutes

Dare to get crazy with pizza night and make some killer, fresh tortillas layered with gooey cheese and delicious beans. Simply follow the Homemade Tortilla Recipe and stuff them chock full of amazing, healthy ingredients.

Ingredients:

4 flour tortillas, made using Victoria Cast Iron tortilla press

1 tablespoon olive oil

1 large onion, diced

1 jalapeno chili, minced (remove seeds and ribs for less heat)

2 garlic cloves, minced

1 teaspoon cumin powder

1/2 teaspoon sea salt

1/2 teaspoon fresh ground pepper

2 (15-ounces) cans black beans, drained and rinsed

1 (12-ounce) bottle of beer, or 1 1/2 cups water

1 (10-ounce) bag frozen corn

2 1/2 cups cheddar cheese, shredded

4 scallions, thinly sliced for garnish

Sour cream, for garnish

Flour Tortillas:

1 cup all-purpose flour

3 teaspoons vegetable shortening, chilled

1/4 teaspoon sea salt

1/2 teaspoon baking powder

1/2 cup water

Sheet of plastic ziploc bag (cut in half)

[please see page 31 for instructions]

Instructions:

1. Preheat oven to 400 degrees Fahrenheit.

2. Lay tortillas on a flat surface. Set a 9-inch springform pan on top of a tortilla. Trim tortillas to fit the pan using a paring knife; repeat until all tortillas are trimmed.

3. Heat olive oil in a large skillet over medium-high heat. Add onion, jalapeno, garlic, cumin powder, salt and pepper. Cook 5-7 minutes, stirring occasionally, until softened.

4. Add beans. Gently fold in beer, and bring to a boil. Reduce heat to medium and simmer, 8-10 minutes, until liquid has nearly evaporated.

5. Stir in corn and scallions. Remove from heat.

6. Place one tortilla in the bottom of springform pan. Cover with 1/4 of the beans and 1/2 cup of cheese. Top with a tortilla and repeat three times. Layer top tortilla with 1 cup of cheese.

7. Bake for 20 to 25 minutes, until cheese is melted. Remove the sides of the pan. Garnish pie with scallions. Slice into wedges and serve with a dollop of sour cream on the side.

Nutritional Info: Calories: 1210 | Sodium: 704 mg | Dietary Fiber: 36.8 g | Total Fat: 31.3 g | Total Carbs: 166.4 g | Protein: 68.0 g.

Tortilla S'mores

Servings: 3-6 | Prep Time: 5 minutes | Cook Time: 3 minutes

If you love the campfire treat of classic S'mores, you'll love this Mexican fusion filled version too! For something sinfully sweet when it comes to family outings, Tortilla S'mores are just the thing to get the kids in on the cooking action. Try serving them up for afternoon snacks or some play date fun with friends.

Ingredients:

3 flour tortillas, cut in half; made using Victoria Cast Iron tortilla press

1 bag of mini marshmallows

1 bar of ibarra mexican chocolate

Aluminum foil

Flour Tortillas

1 cup all-purpose flour

3 teaspoons vegetable shortening, chilled

1/4 teaspoon sea salt

1/2 teaspoon baking powder

1/2 cup water

Sheet of plastic ziploc bag (cut in half)

[please see page 31 for instructions]

Instructions:

1. Lay the Ibarra on a cutting board, and coarsely chop into 1 inch chunks.
2. Place a few pieces of chocolate in the middle of half a tortilla. Top each with a handful of mini marshmallows.
3. Wrap each tortilla up like a mini-taco in aluminum foil.
4. Place on a warm grill for about 3 minutes.
5. Remove, unwrap and enjoy!

Nutritional Info: Calories: 254 | Sodium: 46 mg | Dietary Fiber 3.1 g | Total Fat: 8.6g | Total Carbs: 41.0 g | Protein: 4.1 g.

12

Bonus: Pantry

Gluten Free

When it comes to eating gluten free, there are a few things you might think are gluten free, but are indeed not gluten free. The ingredients below can be used to substitute for items in recipes above.

Gluten-free Taco Seasoning, like McCormick. You'd be super surprised how many companies use gluten products to beef up those seasoning packets.

Use corn tortillas in lieu of flour as masa harina is naturally gluten free.

Paleo & Non-Dairy

Some of the recipes above call for cheese and dairy, so how do you swap them out?

- Daiya Shreds - Cheddar, Mozzarella, Pepper Jack
- Daiya Blocks - Jalapeno Havarti, Cheddar, Monterey Jack
- Daiya Cream Cheese
- Coconut Milk
- Almond Milk
- Soy Milk
- Follow Your Heart Vegan Egg - plant based egg replacement
- Earth Balance Buttery Spread
- Tofutti Dairy Free Sour Cream
- Follow Your Heart Vegan Gourmet Sour Cream
- So Delicious Dairy Free Plain Greek Yogurt

Deliciously Random, Amazing Ingredients

Fill your pantry with delicious mexican spices, sauces, cheeses and creams. Choose the style and amount of heat you want to add to one of the recipes above by swapping out jalapenos for a chocolate habanero or ghost pepper. No matter which way you want to flavor your mexican-style food, these ingredients are great to have on hand with your Victoria Cast Iron tortilla press.

- Adobo Seasoning
- Barbacoa Rub
- Chorizo Seasoning
- Habanero Mango
- Manzanillo Seasoning
- Mole Seasoning
- Ancho flakes
- Chipotle "Morita" Flakes
- Crushed Habanero Flakes
- Cumin powder
- Chipotle powder
- Smoked Paprika
- Garlic powder
- Oregano
- Saffron
- Ancho Chiles in Adobo Sauce
- Mole sauce
- Green chilies
- Tomatillos
- Cilantro
- Hominy
- Napalitos
- Refried Beans
- Chorizo
- Piquillo Peppers
- Sweet Piquant Peppers
- Peeled Pimentos
- Habanero Peppers
- Ghost Peppers
- Jalapeno Peppers
- Poblano Peppers
- Chocolate Habanero Peppers
- Wiltshire Chili Farm Chipotle Chili Salt
- Queso Oaxaca
- Queso Cotija
- Crema Mexicana

Next Steps...

DID YOU ENJOY THE BOOK?

IF SO, THEN LET ME KNOW BY LEAVING A REVIEW ON AMAZON! Reviews are the lifeblood of independent authors. I would appreciate even a few words and rating if that's all you have time for. Here's the link:

http://www.healthyhappyfoodie.org/aa1-freebooks

IF YOU DID NOT LIKE THIS BOOK, THEN PLEASE TELL ME! Email me at feedback@HHFpress.com and let me know what you didn't like! Perhaps I can change it. In today's world a book doesn't have to be stagnant, it can improve with time and feedback from readers like you. You can impact this book, and I welcome your feedback. Help make this book better for everyone!

DO YOU LIKE FREE BOOKS?

Every month we release a new book, and we offer it to our current readers first...absolutely free! This helps us get early feedback before launching a book, and lets you stock your shelf full of interesting and valuable books for free!

Some recent titles include:

- The Complete Vegetable Spiralizer Cookbook
- My Lodge Cast Iron Skillet Cookbook
- 101 The New Crepes Cookbook

To receive this month's free book, just go to

http://www.healthyhappyfoodie.org/aa1-freebooks